EARLY
CHRISTIAN THOUGHT
AND THE CLASSICAL
TRADITION

EARLY CHRISTIAN THOUGHT AND THE CLASSICAL TRADITION

Studies in Justin
Clement, and Origen

BY

HENRY CHADWICK

Oxford   New York

OXFORD UNIVERSITY PRESS

Oxford University Press, Walton Street, Oxford OX2 6DP

Oxford New York Toronto
Delhi Bombay Calcutta Madras Karachi
Kuala Lumpur Singapore Hong Kong Tokyo
Nairobi Dar es Salaam Cape Town
Melbourne Auckland Madrid

and associated companies in
Berlin Ibadan

Oxford is a trade mark of Oxford University Press

Published in the United States
by Oxford University Press Inc., New York

British Library Cataloguing in Publication Data
Chadwick, Henry
Early Christian thought and the classical tradition.
1. Greece—Intellectual life 2. Christianity and other
religions—Greek.
I. Title
180 BR128.G8
ISBN 0–19–826673–1

7 9 10 8

Printed in Great Britain
on acid-free paper by
The Ipswich Book Co. Ltd., Suffolk

PREFACE

THIS book is based mainly on the Hewett Lectures on early Alexandrian Christianity, delivered in 1962 at Union Theological Seminary, New York, at Andover Newton Theological School, and at the Episcopal Theological School, Cambridge, Massachusetts. The substratum of the book consists of the words then spoken in the lecture room, though with revisions and enlargements. To this spoken discourse I have ventured to append annotations which in a few instances may seem to go ill with a text addressed to a more general audience, but may nevertheless, I hope, be found to contain something of interest for those readers for whom the stuff of a book consists in the notes and marginalia.

It is a pleasure to express my cordial gratitude both to the Trustees of the Hewett Lectureship for their invitation and to my most generous and friendly hosts at the three colleges for the surpassing kindness of their welcome. I have also to thank my brother Martin Chadwick for help in removing some stylistic asperities.

H. C.

CONTENTS

1. THE VINDICATION OF CHRISTIANITY   1

2. THE LIBERAL PURITAN   31

3. THE ILLIBERAL HUMANIST   66

4. THE PERENNIAL ISSUE   95

1

THE VINDICATION OF CHRISTIANITY

IN a famous passage of high rhetoric Tertullian puts a question that has reverberated down the centuries in the history of Western thought. 'What', he asks, 'has Athens to do with Jerusalem?'[1] For his contemporary Clement of Alexandria and his junior Origen, the answer is 'Much every way'. For they represent a coming together of the categories of Biblical and Hellenic thinking, a synthesis which leaves an indelible mark on subsequent theology. But their positive answer to the question was not that given by every Christian at the end of the second century, and it would be quite wrong to suppose only ignorant and uneducated believers returned a negative reply. Tertullian may have been an extremist—the kind of person who is happiest when advocating the cause of a small dissenting minority— but he was no fool, and he presupposes that the correct and indeed the only true answer to his question is 'Nothing whatever'. He wishes to assert an absolute and radical discontinuity between Christianity and philosophy: to mix them up means to allow pagan thinking to dictate terms to the gospel or to invite an incoherent, gnostic amalgam of the two which will satisfy neither true believers nor true philosophers. So Tertullian's interest here is to preserve the distinctiveness of faith, to prevent it from becoming absorbed within a suffocating system of metaphysical speculation where it has no room to breathe. Tertullian sees Christianity as flinging down a gage of challenge to philosophy. To reduce it all to sweet reasonableness is to miss its supernatural character, and therefore his ultimate Christian confession is the grinding paradox 'I believe it because it is absurd'.[2] (We must not, of course, take too literally Tertullian's shrill rhetoric, but it is clear that his notorious utterance is a milestone along a path in Christian thought which leads through Sir Thomas Browne to Kierkegaard and his modern disciples.)

But the theology of paradox is not the only possible account of the relation between faith and reason. Elsewhere Tertullian does not always speak in such robust terms of the unbridgeable chasm separating Athens and Jerusalem. He was as well educated as anyone of his time: a competent lawyer, able to publish his writings in both Latin and Greek with equal facility, sufficiently acquainted with the current ideas and arguments of the Platonic, Stoic, and Aristotelian schools and also possessing some knowledge of medicine.[3] He recognized that Christianity needed the language of reasoned discourse to interpret its doctrines of Incarnation and Trinity. He loved to discern an unreflective but genuine embryonic feeling after God in the intuitive and often casual utterances of ordinary people, expressing an innate awareness of God, which show how beneath the encrusting prejudices imposed by the customs and habits

of society the soul is 'anima naturaliter Christiana'.[4]
Here we have a very different way of thinking from the
blazing paradoxes of his more aggressive moods. According to this line of approach Christianity is the full
development of something already potentially present
in the human soul. Grace makes explicit what in nature
is implicit.

Latin-speaking Christianity in the West did not ac-
quire a philosophical mind of any considerable quality
before the middle of the fourth century, with the conversion of the Roman Neoplatonist Marius Victorinus,
to whose difficult and reputedly obscure writings Augustine was to owe a little in constructing his own synthesis
of Christianity and Platonism. But in the Greek East the
philosophical question was being faced much earlier.

The beginnings of the encounter go right back into
the New Testament itself. The story begins no doubt
with St. Paul's speech at Athens, an incident evidently
invested with high symbolic importance for the author
of Acts; and in the letters of the apostle whose method
it was to be all things to all men we can see a masterly
attempt to retranslate the Palestinian gospel into the
religious idiom of the surrounding world. In the pro-
logue to St. John's gospel, the Word, who is God's self-
revelation, is not only incarnate in Christ. He is also the
light who lightens every man coming into the world,
and is the principle of rationality and order in the cosmos and in mankind. Here already we are meeting the
tension between the concept of a natural or general
revelation of God given to all men endowed with reason

(and presumably apparent especially in men whose rational powers are most highly developed) and a unique act of God in a chosen person, in the Word made flesh. The particularity of the Incarnation is the way by which the universality of God's creative providence is known and understood. Conversely, God's universal care for his creatures makes intelligible and reasonable the particular care manifest in redemption.

These apostolic hints of the shape of things to come so strikingly foreshadow the developments of Greek theology in the second and third centuries that there is always a strong temptation to think of St. John as the founding father of the Christian development of Logos theology in the Greek apologists from Justin Martyr onwards. This temptation must be resisted. The case for regarding the fourth gospel as an apologia to the non-Jewish world is not very strong. And in Justin we find a theologian on whom no real Johannine influence is discernible. While it is more probable than not that he knew the fourth gospel,[5] it is evident that characteristically Johannine themes did nothing to shape the essential pattern of his thinking. So we have the strange paradox that the man chiefly responsible for making the Logos idea at home in Christian theology was little influenced by St. John. It is not even certain that he had read Philo.

In the New Testament, then, we can trace anticipations of the way ahead. But they are not more than hints. The New Testament writers do not philosophize, and we may think this a fact of providential importance since in consequence the gospel is not inextricably associated with a first-century metaphysical structure. Its relationship to philosophy has therefore a detachment which is to the clear advantage of both sides.[6] At the same time the detachment is never absolute; for while the Christian faith may not require a specific metaphysical framework for its proper self-expression, this does not mean that it is able to live in a happy and lifelong union with any intellectual position whatsoever. In the Church Fathers, and especially in Clement and Origen, we see Christianity working out its metaphysical salvation, partly in dependence upon, but partly also in criticism of, classical Greek philosophies.

In the first and second centuries the philosophy with which the Christians had to come to terms, the philosophy taken for granted by ordinary educated folk, was in effect a blend of Stoicism and Platonism. Sceptical and empirical philosophers existed of course; their rationalistic arguments against the myths of polytheism and against the authenticity of divination were an invaluable arsenal on which the Christians freely and gladly drew. But the prevailing mood was more positive. On the ethical side it was profoundly moulded by Stoicism with its ideal of the 'wise man' untouched and unmoved by all outward calamities, knowing that, provided he is captain of his soul, none can harm him against his will. On the metaphysical side it looked more to Platonism with its picture of man as belonging in his inner being to a higher world but during this life imprisoned in a physical body. The diffused popular philosophy taken by educated people, without specialist responsibility or knowledge, as the source of their guiding principles was an eclectic affair, not bound within either the straitjacket of school orthodoxy or the requirements of rigid internal consistency.

As early as Philo, we see that the current intellectual coin of the more literate classes of society is this blend of Stoic ethics with Platonic metaphysics and some Aristotelian logic. Like the form of Greek spoken in the hellenistic world, it is a philosophical *koine*, and Philo simply takes it for granted. As a learned Jew he is committed to a hellenized Judaism which remains strict about observance though it may often be liberal in belief. For him the Pentateuch's narratives and laws are a symbolist allegory, an antique Jewish cryptogram, full of strictly modern Greek ethics and metaphysics which the illuminated exegete can discern and explicate. At the same time it is the positive and independent task of philosophy to prepare the soul for the scriptural revelation and to be 'the handmaid' of theology.

Philo was applying to the Pentateuch the methods of allegorical exegesis which contemporary philosophers had long been freely applying to Homer and to the ancient myths of the gods. It was widely agreed that the apparently crude myths of the poets really contained inspired allegories about the cosmos and the place of man in it. Similar mysteries could also be discovered in the myths of the Oriental cults such as the religion of Mithras the sun-god, or of Attis and Cybele, or of Isis and Osiris, or of the Syrian Goddess. An orthodox Jew like Philo could not, of course, agree to putting the Law of Moses on a level with the myths of Greece, Egypt, and Persia. He could accept eclecticism in philosophy, but not syncretism in myth and cult, against which he utters sharp warnings. A liberal Jew, however, might not find the mixing of myths an intellectual impossibility; and on the hellenistic side syncretizers were very willing to incorporate Jewish elements in their scheme by the usual method of identifying the God of the Jews with some familiar figure like Dionysus, for example, or Saturn.[7]

The belief that all religions are equally true, because all are myths symbolizing the same basic and ultimate verities, receives one of its most characteristic expressions in Gnosticism, that sombre and repellent theosophy in which Christian redemption is fused with a pessimistic interpretation of Plato, a dualism drawn from a hellenized version of Zoroastrianism, important elements from heterodox Judaism, the whole being mingled with astrology and with magic as the principal technique for overcoming the powers of fate.

The fact that the initial syntheses between the Christian gospel and the ideas of the hellenistic world were on the side of religion and mysticism meant that the Christian mission on Gentile soil was haunted by Gnosticism virtually from the start. St. Paul's epistles to Corinth and Colossae already reveal the immediate development of a dualistic Gnosticism. Even at this very early stage we meet the gnostic claim to a higher, non-rational knowledge of truths profounder than those apprehended at the level of simple faith; and from the epistle to the Colossians it is clear that the heretical teachers combated by the apostle were appealing to philosophy to justify their claims. 'Beware', he replies, 'lest anyone delude you by philosophy or vain deceit.'[8]

The immediate effect of the gnostic crisis within the Church was to make many members of it acutely defensive about anything intellectual. If the heretics appealed to philosophy, then philosophy must be vain deceit, human speculation rather than revealed truth. The influence of this negative attitude persisted for a long period (it enjoyed a sharp revival in the fourth century with Epiphanius of Salamis) and created the main problem to which Clement of Alexandria addressed himself. Looking back on the second century with the advantage and detachment of hindsight we can see how natural and easy it was for Christians to conclude from the gnostic propaganda that philosophy must be of the devil. If the gnostic claim had any truth, it was 'the mother of heresy'. Hippolytus constructs his refutation of the heretical sects on the assumption that each sect has corrupted the true faith by following the principles of some philosopher. We may notice in passing that the pagan philosophers themselves were not much impressed by the gnostic claim that Plato justified their position. It is true that Gnosticism made some headway within Neoplatonic circles, but it provoked an impassioned attack by Plotinus which is one of the finest sections of the so-called Enneads.[9] In the Church itself the anti-intellectualist reaction provoked by the heretics was not in the long run anything like as important as the considered intellectual reply that they made necessary. Irenaeus, for example, devotes his second book to a demonstration that the gnostic systems are irrational and incoherent, inconsistent with their own presuppositions as well as contrary to all common sense. Irenaeus appeals to reason and hard argument. So, although the short-term effect of gnostic propaganda was to make many believers fearful of philosophical speculations, it remains true to say that the Church rejected the Gnostics because they used reason too little rather than because they used it too much. For in rejecting the gnostic way the Christians thereby rejected as an inauthentic adulteration and corruption any theology of pure revelation teaching salvation by an arbitrary predestination of the elect and the total depravity of the lost, and possessing no criteria of rational judgement. In any event, the Church could not escape reasoned argument if it was ever to explain itself and so extend its mission to the world. A preacher in any age called to address himself to trained minds cannot be content to assert and to reiterate, like the Bellman in Lewis Carroll's *Hunting of the Snark* whose principle was 'What I tell you three times is true'.

Clement and Origen were not the first educated Christians to meet the philosophical question. The way had been mapped out in advance by the second-century apologists, above all by Justin Martyr who is certainly the greatest of them besides being the most voluminous.

Since it is he more than anyone else who constructs the platform upon which Clement and Origen will stand, he must detain us for a space. His biography is quickly outlined. Born of Greek parents near Samaria early in the second century, he drifted to Ephesus where, like many other young men, he went the rounds of the philosophical teachers—Stoic, Peripatetic, Pythagorean, and finally Platonist. Meditating one day in solitude by the sea-shore he met an old man who refuted his Platonism and then told him of the prophets predicting the coming of Christ. Justin was converted. He became a professed teacher of 'the Christian philosophy' and left Ephesus for Rome. After further travels he returned to Rome and died a martyr's death there some time between 162 and 168. We have from his pen three works of certain authenticity,[10] preserved in a solitary independent manuscript, dated 1364, now at Paris: the 'First Apology' addressed to the emperor Antoninus Pius, the long 'Dialogue with Trypho', unhappily not complete, and the 'Second Apology' which is a manifesto (probably supplementing the 'First Apology') issued at a critical time at Rome when the city prefect has been persecuting the Church and a Cynic philosopher named Crescens has been vigorously attacking their beliefs. All three works, including the Dialogue with the Jew, are intended for a Gentile or Gentile-Christian public.

Of all the early Christian theologians Justin is the most optimistic about the harmony of Christianity and Greek philosophy. For him the gospel and the best elements in Plato and the Stoics are almost identical ways of apprehending the same truth. Towards pagan cult and religious myth Justin is sharply negative; polytheism is crude, superstitious, and often immoral—a demonic counterfeit and caricature of the true religion[11] put about by evil powers to deceive men into supposing the gospel to be just one more religious myth of the usual sort,[12] and riveting men down to idols to prevent their minds rising to anything higher.[13] His typical examples of paganism at its worst are the Egyptian cult of animals and the immoral orgies accompanying the worship of Antinous, the deified favourite of Hadrian drowned as a young man in the Nile in 130.[14] But towards philosophy Justin could hardly be more positive and generous. Admittedly the Greek philosophers made serious errors. The various schools have seen different aspects of the truth; hence their disagreements with one another.[15] The Stoics are first-rate on ethics, but disastrously wrong in their materialism, pantheism, and fatalism.[16] They are feeling dimly after the truth in their doctrine that the cosmos is liable to periodical catastrophes by floods and conflagrations. The last catastrophe was the flood of Deucalion (whom Justin, like Philo, identifies with the Biblical Noah). The next, they say, will be the cosmic conflagration when everything is dissolved into fire. This, declares Justin, is an echo of the eschatological fire of God's judgement.[17]

The philosophers who in Justin's estimate stand nearest to Christianity are the Platonists. Between the two positions there is no gulf fixed so great that the passage from one to the other is impossible or unnatural. For a Platonist to accept Christianity, as Justin himself has done, is no revolutionary step involving a radical rejection of his earlier world-view.[18] Socrates saw that the old myths of the gods were false and corrupting, and in his death he was a martyr for the truth, a pattern of integrity for Christian martyrs.[19] Plato was right in teaching that God is transcendent and is not in space, but is immutable, impassible, incorporeal, and nameless.[20] He was also correct in the myth of the *Timaeus* which declares that the world is 'created'.[21] (It should, however, be noted that at times Justin uses language suggesting that Creation was the ordering of a pre-existent matter, a view explicitly held by his successor Athenagoras; but Justin does not express himself with complete clarity on the point, and the apparent unselfconsciousness with which he uses these ambiguous phrases suggests that he had not thought the problem out, rather than that he deliberately avoided the question'.)[22] Plato, he continues, was also right about the soul's kinship to God and possession of free will, and about punishment after death.[23] In some things Plato was wrong, as for example in supposing that the soul possesses a natural and inherent immortality by its own nature rather than in dependence upon the creative will of God; and he erred again in believing that the soul suffers transmigration.[24] But at least Socrates realized the need for a divine revelation when he declared that it is hard to find the Maker of the universe and unsafe to declare him when found.[25]

Justin not only affirms the dissemination of the truth among the Greek philosophers but also provides a positive theory to account for the phenomenon. Similarities between Christianity and paganism in worship or myth are explained as imitations of the truth inspired by the devil, who with foresight and sagacity has thereby tried to inoculate men against the gospel by caricatures of the Incarnation or of the virgin birth or of baptism and the eucharist.[26] There can be no reconciliation with counterfeit ideas of worship. It is on this ground that Justin consistently resists all pagan invitations to a religious syncretism which merges the Christian story with Greek legends. But the higher philosophical truths about God were not acquired by pagan philosophers through any diabolical agency. They came from wholly respectable sources: either by derivation from the writings of Moses or through the exercise of the divinely given reason.

The remote antiquity of Moses was a long-established theme of apologetic in the hellenistic synagogues. At the beginning of the second century Josephus wrote a reply to critics of his *Antiquities* and also to current anti-Semitic prejudices—the work usually entitled 'Against Apion'. It contains elaborate calculations to prove the hoary antiquity of the Jews and the dependence of Greek civilization upon them. Likewise Philo's massive expositions of the Pentateuch presuppose that Plato and the Greek philosophers were dependent on Moses, who had subtly composed his patriarchal narratives and ceremonial laws as a veil for the deepest philosophical, moral, and religious insights. If we ask how this literary dependence can have come about, an answer lay ready to hand. According to Plato's biographers he had at one time visited Egypt;[27] perhaps he had actually read a copy of the Pentateuch left behind by Moses or had at least made contact with learned commentators on it.[28]

The bizarre notion is one for which we may find it hardly possible to suppress a pitying smile, and it is, of course, absurd. (It sounds too much like the quaint claim that the Greeks derived their culture from Ghana, or that St. Paul founded the Church of England on his roundabout route to Spain.) It might be observed that among the Church Fathers the argument had its critics: in the *City of God* Augustine gently comments on the improbability of the theory.[29] But it must also be recognized that from a strictly historical viewpoint our superior smile is a grossly unimaginative anachronism. In the age of the Antonines no one would have thought it a preposterous or contemptible thesis, even if he did not happen to think it probable. The contemporary Neopythagoreans, for instance, had had considerable success in representing Plato as the great popularizer of Pythagorean doctrines, finding their theology especially in the *Timaeus* and the *Parmenides* and producing pseudepigraphic texts in which very early Pythagoreans expounded Platonism.[30] And in the biographies of Plato it stood written that Plato had visited the Pythagorean schools in southern Italy. So no grotesque extravagance could reasonably be discerned in the claim that Plato popularized for a Greek public the esoteric teachings of Moses. At least one Neopythagorean accepted outright the Jewish-Christian claim: Numenius of Apamea, contemporary of Justin and precursor in important respects of Plotinus and Neoplatonism, affirms the theory of dependence without qualification: 'What is Plato', he asks, 'but Moses in Attic Greek?'[31] Plotinus's follower Amelius supposes that St. John had derived his Logos language from his study of the obscure sayings of Heraclitus.[32] (For Celsus see below, p. 23.)

In Justin's disciple Tatian and in Clement of Alexandria we find the theory of dependence formulated in sharply polemical form: it is denounced as 'theft' and 'plagiarism'. But in Justin the argument has no anti-Hellenic edge. He does not accuse the Greeks of failing properly to acknowledge their borrowings or of corrupting the divine revelation by introducing stupid misunderstandings. That the Greeks borrowed from Moses is for Justin a singular merit, not at all an unethical proceeding. On the contrary, so sharp was Plato's intelligence that according to Justin he was able to deduce from some uncommonly obscure hints in the Pentateuch the idea of a divine Triad of supreme beings.[33] Naturally Justin's remarks here are of the greatest interest as foreshadowing the coming together of the Christian Trinity with that of Neoplatonism.

In this connexion we may notice a crucial point, that the Platonic doctrine of God's transcendence is assumed and exploited for controversial purposes by Justin when he is arguing against Trypho the Jew that Christ is the pre-existent divine Logos. It is Justin's thesis in the

Dialogue that the God who appeared to the patriarchs in the Old Testament theophanies must be the Logos-Son.[34] He cannot be the supreme Father since he is too far removed to have direct contact with this inferior realm and cannot have abandoned his universal care for the cosmos as a whole to become circumscribed by incarnation in one small corner of the world.[35] The thesis here advanced was destined to have a highly successful future in later theology until the end of the fourth century by which time it had at long last become apparent that the presuppositions of the argument led with a virtually irresistible force straight to Arianism. Not until Augustine's *de Trinitate* did theology succeed in getting rid of it.[36] I venture to emphasise this point, for the argument is Justin's one major dependence upon Greek philosophy in a matter of real substance, a point where his Platonism is directly providing the basic presuppositions of his theology, and it must be pronounced a *faux pas* for which his successors had to pay a high price in blood and tears.

Justin's second ground for affirming the positive value of philosophy is that all rational beings share in the universal Logos or Reason who is Christ. So both Abraham and Socrates were 'Christians before Christ'.[37] So also the noble morality of the Stoics comes from their share in the 'seminal Logos', the divine Reason who has sown the seeds of truth in all men as beings created in God's image.[38] Accordingly the philosophers have been able to read God both in the book of nature and in the inner deliverances of their reason. Justin loves to find the footprints of God in the non-Christian order and in nature. A ship's mast, for example, or the human form, or even the standards of the Roman army can remind him of the mystery of the Cross (a striking foreshadowing of Constantine's *labarum*!).[39]

Justin does not merely make Socrates a Christian. His Christ is a philosopher, 'no sophist',[40] but a genuine teacher of the way to 'happiness' (*eudaimonia*),[41] in himself the personification of 'right reason' (*orthos logos*) teaching 'divine virtue'.[42] His teaching in the Sermon on the Mount is wholly in line with natural law; it is a universal morality, valid for all races and stripped of the national particularism of Judaism.[43]

Nevertheless, there is nothing reduced about Justin's estimate of the person of Christ. Christ, he declares, is not only man but God.[44] Whereas Socrates confessed acute difficulty in finding God and speaking about him, Christ actually revealed God. No one was ever martyred for his faith in Socrates. Moreover, while Socrates addressed only the intelligent, believers in Christ include not only philosophers but also uneducated and illiterate folk who have been able to grasp divine truth without training in logic.[45] Justin's contrast is in effect that of the natural and the supernatural. Christianity, he says, is divine where philosophy is human; it is certain where philosophy can only guess.[46] For Christ is a power of the ineffable Father. He transcends the natural order of reason, and speaks with the power of God.[47] The supernatural character of his achievement is proved by his miracles, by the amazing fulfilment of ancient prophecies in his life, death, and resurrection, and by the rapid extension of the gospel throughout the world to reach every race.[48] The truth of the gospel is a matter of ocular demonstration.[49] In fact, that a crucified man is Son of the supreme God and Judge of all mankind is a proposition so wildly improbable that we should never have come to believe it unless we had been moved by compelling witness.[50]

Justin is so warm and positive in his evaluation of Greek philosophy that one might expect him simply to take an eclectic Platonism as his prior framework and to fit into this given structure as many features of Christianity as he can. Nothing could be further from the facts. It is an expression of the optimism and extrovert confidence of Justin's programme for harmony and co-operation between faith and reason that there is nothing whatever in the traditional pattern of Christian teaching which he feels it necessary to explain away or even to mute.

Experience has made us think of 'apologists' as if they were like those commercial public relations officers who are exposed to such insidious temptations to present a glossy front to the world and who only appear when they are needed to cover up weak points in the precarious case they are paid to plead. Justin, on the contrary, is utterly frank and open-hearted, and his lack of reserve is especially striking when we consider that the pattern of theology as he has received it is wholly free from any breath of demythologization. Although he never sets out to give a single, succinct statement of his beliefs, it is possible to piece together a mosaic providing a clear and surprisingly full account of his doctrines of God, Creation, Incarnation, Atonement, the Church, the sacraments of baptism and eucharist, and the Last Things. In a word, every essential element in the traditional Christian pattern could be expounded on the basis of Justin's statements and allusions, together with some other elements that may be thought less essential. For his opposition to Gnosticism leads him to insist not only on a full-blooded and extremely literalistic doctrine of the resurrection of the flesh but also on a strictly earthly hope for a millennial reign of Christ at Jerusalem[51] such as neither Clement nor Origen could possibly have defended except as poetic and symbolic language.[52] There is no sign in Justin of any tendency to mitigate or to attenuate traditional beliefs, above all, his doctrines of Creation, revelation in history, and eschatology, in order to meet philosophical criticism.

Justin is utterly convinced of the ultimate oneness of Christ with the highest Reason. It is coherent with this that he is the earliest exponent of the view that the two principal barriers to conversion are prejudice and misinformation.[53] Throughout his writings he invariably assumes that once the Christian position has been properly set out by an intelligent man, once its way of life has been seen in a faithful disciple, and once it has been seriously attended to by a sincere and open mind, the fulfilment of these three conditions can have only one consequence: the truth will be manifest and forthwith accepted. 'I have no need', he writes, 'of any sophistical ingenuity, but only to be candid and frank.'[54]

I have ventured to dwell at some length on Justin because he is vital to the comprehension of later developments, and because he is easy to underestimate. At first sight he seems a simple enough person, straightforward and unsophisticated, perhaps even innocent. But it is important for Church historians (and not only for them) to distinguish between innocence and stupidity. Justin is a plain man, but he is not stupid; he can be shown to ·be as competent an expounder of Platonism as his contemporaries,[55] and, despite his rambling style, is very far from being an ignorant or half-educated fool. For us, however, he claims attention for a more profound reason. What is central in his thought is the way in which the Biblical doctrine of God and his relation to the world provides him with a criterion of judgement, in the light of which he evaluates the great names in the history of Greek philosophy. Justin does not merely use Greek philosophy. He passes judgement upon it. His position may be made plain by contrasting him with two pagan contemporaries, Lucian of Samosata and Numenius of Apamea. Lucian is a 'rationalist' in the loose, negative sense of being wholly cynical about all traditional religion; but he is equally cynical about philosophy. He confronts the would-be philosopher with the existence of rival and incompatible schools, observes that life is too short to examine them all properly, and so draws the defeatist conclusion that a decision in favour of one rather than another is arbitrary and irrational. Which of them is true is 'mere guesswork', and Lucian does not conceal his own view that the different schools are only right in so far as they assert their rivals to be mistaken.[56] By contrast Numenius is as far from Lucian's weary disillusionment as possible. His aim is to achieve a synthesis of all philosophies and all religions. For him, therefore, everyone is right, and everything is true. There can be no criterion of judgement by which Numenius is prepared to reject anything, and his intellectual affinities are in certain respects with the Gnostics.[57]

Justin stands between Lucian and Numenius. He knows what is true and judges accordingly. So with regard to the doctrine of God, he declares that the Stoics are wrong. Pantheism, materialism, and fatalism are false. But the Stoics are excellent on morality. Plato, on the other hand, though right about God's transcendence and incorporeality, is wrong in his doctrine of the soul and in his acceptance of the cyclic, fatalistic theory of transmigration. In all these judgements we see Justin's Christian faith impelling him to reject metaphysical positions that he thinks incompatible with the Bible.[58]

It is on this ground that Justin must be asserted to have some measure of genuinely independent status as a thinker. It is a naïve mistake to suppose that because the diffused philosophy of his time was eclectic, inserting Stoic ethics into a framework of Platonic metaphysics, Justin is *merely* reflecting this popular synthesis in his view that Plato was mainly right about metaphysics and the Stoics about ethics. Precisely what one means by the misty term 'eclecticism' it is never very easy to say. There is no philosophy that does not draw together elements from diverse sources. But if eclecticism merely means a kind of weak intellectual syncretism without any principle of judgement (such as that exemplified by Numenius), endeavouring to harmonize differing positions with the prime end of achieving concord rather than discord, and compromise rather than truth, then it is clear that Justin does not fit into this category.

The outstretched hand of sympathy which Justin extended to his intellectual opponents, and especially to the Platonists, was received with neither enthusiasm nor gratitude. Some fifteen or twenty years later the Platonist Celsus wrote his well-known attack on Christianity, most of which we can read in the quotations preserved in Origen's elaborate reply; there is a strong case for thinking that Celsus had read some Christian apologetic writing, and that he may well have been especially provoked by Justin.[59] The Platonist absolutely rejects the Christian notion that in pagan philosophy there is a partial apprehension of truths more completely found in Christianity, that Plato is either a branch derived from Moses or an immature stage on the way towards the perfect fulfilment in Christianity. There are, he freely recognizes, affinities. Both Plato and Jesus teach humility,[60] non-resistance to evil,[61] and that opulence is an obstacle to the good life.[62] Platonism too teaches that the supreme heaven is the final destiny of worthy souls,[63] and distinguishes between divine and human wisdom.[64] But the explanation of these affinities is not that Plato had read Moses. The dependence is rather the other way round—Jesus had read Plato and Paul had studied Heraclitus.[65] Christianity (Celsus urges) is a corruption of the primordial truths enshrined in the ancient polytheistic tradition.[66] It is a break-away movement[67] from Judaism[68] which was itself the creation of a radical revolutionary figure, Moses, who led the Jews to revolt from their original home in Egypt[69] and taught them to believe monotheism and to reject the old polytheism.[70] Judaism Celsus cordially dislikes;[71] but he concedes that whatever peculiarities it may have it has at least the merit of being national and traditional, whereas Christianity has no tradition and claims proselytes of all races and peoples.[72] For Celsus it is axiomatic that nothing can be both new and true.[73] Christianity is a corruption of Greek ideas with nothing individual or fresh to say in the ethical sphere[74] and with strange doctrines derived from misunderstandings of the sound polytheistic tradition in so far as they have any measure of truth in them.[75]

So Celsus reverses Justin's arguments. Where Justin had suggested that the Greek doctrine of periodic floods and conflagrations was a misunderstanding of what the Bible says about Noah's flood and the coming fire of judgement, Celsus retorts that on the contrary it is the Christians who have misunderstood the Greeks. Noah's flood is borrowed from the myth of Deucalion.[76] The notion of the fire of God's judgement is a corruption of the truth of the great cosmic conflagration[77] (which is all part of the natural process, not an arbitrary act).[78] Celsus draws up a list of parallels between the Bible and the philosophers to prove that everything true in Christian teaching is a direct borrowing, and that every partial or faint resemblance is the consequence of misunderstanding.[79] If an explanation of Christian error is sought, Celsus has a quick answer: the majority of Christians are stupid.[80] Origen very reasonably replies to this that the membership of the Church is a cross-section of society and that the proportion of educated believers in the Church roughly corresponds to the proportion of educated people in society as a whole.[81] But for Celsus the dull-wittedness of the majority of Christians is more than an accidental fact; for him it is symptomatic of the inherently irrational and anti-intellectual character which he ascribes to Christianity as such.[82]

Celsus's unflattering portrait of the Church and its theology so ignores the existence of educated believers that the conclusion has sometimes been drawn that he could not have known the work of the Apologists.[83] The conclusion is mistaken because it ignores the manifest signs of determination with which Celsus shuts his eyes to the fact of a rational Christian theology. There is an emotional heat apparent in his dogged insistence on the anti-cultural nature of Christianity. In fact, he is well aware of Christians who vindicate their claims for Jesus by appeals to his miracles and to the fulfilment of prophecy,[84] who describe Christ as the 'Logos', and who use sceptical arguments against traditional paganism such as the tomb of Zeus in Crete.[85] He admits that there are intelligent Christians 'able to explain away crudities' but dismisses them as clever knaves driven to allegory because they are ashamed of the Old Testament and adroitly rationalizing a barbarian superstition.[86] The real heart of Christianity, as he sees it, is as hostile to the whole Greek tradition of rational investigation as it is to the Greek religious and cultic tradition. So Christianity is not merely a religious revolution with profound social and political consequences; it is essentially hostile to all positive human values. The Christians say (he accuses), 'Do not ask questions, only believe'. They say, 'Wisdom is foolishness with God'.[87] Put embarrassing questions about the resurrection of the body, and they will flee to that last refuge of the intellectually destitute, 'Anything is possible to God'.[88] They claim that divine revelation is validated as such by its transcendence of common reason; but there are many rival claimants to revelation—if we may not judge their claims by reason, are we to throw dice to discover which is right?[89]

In Celsus's view the root of the matter lies in the Biblical doctrine of God. The God of both Jews and Christians is a busy, interfering deity.[90] He created this world less than ten thousand years ago.[91] It is all done for the sole benefit of an elect few quite arbitrarily chosen, while everyone else will be consumed by fire in an equally arbitrary destruction of the world.[92] The Christian belief in the Incarnation presupposes that

after an immense period of inactivity God suddenly
wakes up to send his Spirit down to a single individual
in one small corner of the earth, a scandalous particularity which is fatal to any claim for universality.[93] The
very notion of an elect people of God is worse than irrational; it also leads Jews and Christians to imagine that
their myths are superior to everyone else's, and that
their religion is true and all others false. The Jews' belief
that they are God's elect is a mere reflection of inflated
national pride.[94] The idea that God suddenly decides
to make a world and then no less suddenly destroys
it is childish and blasphemous.[95] Moreover, throughout
the process of history the Biblical God is irrationally
intervening. He has to check the evil in the world he
has made (evidently very incompetently)[96] by drastic
interventions like the episode of the tower of Babel or
the Flood or the destruction of Sodom and Gomorrah,[97]
or by frequently sending angels with messages. (In one
place Celsus begins to enumerate the occasions when
angels have been sent, and each one is in his eyes additional evidence for the prosecution.)[98] The Biblical God
is apparently impelled to this strangely capricious behaviour by the feeling that he is neglected by his creatures;
he wants a reluctant humanity to recognize his dignity,
'a very mortal ambition'.[99]

It is not difficult to hear in Celsus's onslaught the
echoes of Marcion's attack upon the Old Testament,
and in fact there is direct evidence that Celsus must
have been familiar with some of the arguments used in
the debate between Marcion and the Church.[100] But it

is not merely the Old Testament God who draws Celsus's obloquy. The New Testament provides the crowning example. The Christian idea of Incarnation is right in line with the Hebraic notion of God as one who intervenes in history, as one who has created by the fiat of his unpredictable will. And the Incarnation is impossible. It means a change in God; and if God changes he must change either for the better or for the worse—either view is incompatible with divine perfection.[101] The fundamental conception of God held by both Jews and Christians is altogether irreconcilable with the principles of Plato.

Again, the Christians attribute transcendent significance to merely contingent facts. For example, they find profound mystical meaning in the Cross as 'the tree of life'. What would they say if Jesus had happened to be strangled or pushed over a cliff? How can they think that an ultimate and eternal significance attaches to events that might have turned out very differently?[102]

Plato had rejected the crude anthropomorphism of the old Greek myths and had spoken of God in impersonal terms. The Christians are appropriating the philosophic criticism of Greek myths, but are largely blind (Celsus thinks) to the crudity of their own myths in Genesis,[103] the imbecilities of which are so embarrassing to intelligent believers that they have to explain them away with forced allegories.[104] How deeply anthropomorphic their conception of God is may be seen in their puerile notion that they cannot 'see' God after death unless they are so resuscitated that the bodily eyes can recover their power of sight.[105]

The 'true doctrine' for Celsus is the Platonic theology that God is unmoved and transcendent, an alpha privative, knowable only by the mind in a strictly dialectical regress pursued until we reach an impersonal ground.[106] God knows no special love for man, still less for an elect few among mankind; he cares for the whole universe in which man is but a small thing.[107] The cosmos does not exist for man any more than it does for dolphins.[108] It just rolls on its everlasting way,[109] and has no anthropocentric purpose or end. It is just there. No special interventions by providence are required, since the amount of evil in the cosmos is constant and determined.[110]

At the same time, this universal providence is regionally exercised by the divine stars[111] and by the inferior deities to whom local cults are offered.[112] The veneration of local gods does not detract from the worship of the supreme God, since they are like satraps or provincial governors representative of the monarch.[113] Indeed, the more local deities are included in the Roman imperial pantheon, the fuller and richer is the honour and worship offered to the transcendent power at the apex of them all.[114] Alternatively, it may also be claimed that it is always one and the same God who is being worshipped in different places under many different names.[115] Celsus is prepared to defend traditional paganism on either basis. His defence is not altogether wholehearted, it is true. His attitude to pagan cult is throughout ambivalent. The old myths of the gods are dissolved into allegory.[116] Much of Celsus's critique of those anthropomorphic elements in the Bible to which he takes such strong objection is an extension to Christianity of the traditional Platonic critique of pagan myth. One form of attack that Celsus often likes to employ is the charge that the Christian story is 'as incredible as' this or that Greek myth which no sensible person believes,[117] or that the Christian eschatology is morally 'no less objectionable than' the fictitious terrors of the mysteries of Dionysus, or that the Christian use of music in worship is 'as emotive and as unscrupulous in its attempts to dull the reason as the techniques used to induce hysterical frenzy by the priests of Cybele'.[118] But such language, critical of both Christianity and paganism, has no radically sceptical basis. It is the expression not of hostility towards religion as such but of an educated and aristocratic contempt for a distressing vulgarity and crudity which, in Celsus's eyes, the Church shares with other Oriental cults. So, for instance, he sees the Christian claims for ecstatic prophecy as typical of a fanaticism commonly found in Phoenicia and Palestine.[119] It is the kind of thing vulgar people do in those places.

Celsus is a religious conservative whose ultimate objection to the Christians is that they have the wrong prejudices. But he is a conservative with an uneasy conscience. He is a polytheist who knows he ought not to be. He is even willing to concede to the Christian attack that there are real dangers in the cult of earth-bound demons who may hold down the soul so that it becomes absorbed in magic and is prevented from rising to a purer and higher religion.[120] He pleads for a 'formal acknowledgement' in cult, but with the significant qualification 'in so far as this is expedient'. Stripped down to its essentials his plea for pagan cult is reducible to the formula 'You can't be too careful'.[121] It is the weakest point in Celsus's armour, and Origen does not fail to observe it in his reply.

Celsus's embarrassment is a measure of the power behind Justin's endeavour to drive a wedge between pagan religion and Greek philosophy and to make common cause with the latter. But for Celsus both philosophy and cult are integral parts of a single indissoluble tradition. He cannot allow Justin to put them asunder. Accordingly at every point where Justin has offered an eirenic programme for the reconciliation of Christianity and eclectic Platonism, Celsus has replied with an impassioned 'No'. In his eyes Christianity is at no point and in no sense continuous with the classical Greek tradition except in so far as it may have borrowed from it and distorted it. The gulf is unbridgeable. Platonism and Stoicism do not point forward to any sort of consummation and fulfilment in Christianity. Christ is not the keystone of an arch formed by Judaism and Hellenism. No such arch exists, and even if it did Celsus would advise the builders to reject the offer of this stone. How can there be harmony between Greek reasoning and the irrational faith of those whose message is 'Commit yourself to God and close your mind'?

In Clement and Origen we shall see how Celsus is answered.

2

THE LIBERAL PURITAN

CLEMENT of Alexandria is not an easy subject for a biographer requiring a coherent chronology and vivid personal details. Eusebius of Caesarea, as always our principal informant for the period of Church history prior to the fourth century, tells us next to nothing about Clement's life except what may be deduced from his surviving writings, especially the trilogy —the *Protrepticus* or 'Exhortation to conversion'; the *Paedagogus* or 'Tutor', a fascinating document of social history intended to provide catechumens and young Christians with instruction in Christian morality and etiquette; and lastly the *Stromateis* or 'Miscellanies', consisting of unsystematic and surprisingly inconsequential notes on a large variety of themes. (At times it seems that Clement is almost anxious that nothing should be too clear.) What emerges unambiguously is Clement's moral and spiritual ideal, and a man's statement of his personal ideal may often be taken to provide a rough self-portrait. Something of Clement's character and personality is therefore reflected in his pages. But otherwise we can say little about him. The only certain date in his biography is that he wrote the first book of the *Stromateis* between 193 and 211.[1] He is generally reticent about himself except at the beginning of the *Stromateis* where, in the course of an elaborate apologia for putting any-thing into writing on such advanced matters as theology, he mentions a number of Christian teachers at whose feet he has sat in Greece, Southern Italy, Syria, and Egypt.[2] Even so he does not tell us their names. The Syrian may have been Justin's pupil Tatian, whose 'Address to the Greeks' Clement especially valued for its learned calculations proving the hoary antiquity of Moses.[3] The last teacher with whom he studied taught in Egypt and was, he says, the greatest of them all. Eusebius gives his name, Pantaenus, a convert from Stoicism, and adds the remarkable information that he had visited India as a missionary and had found Chris-tians there already.[4] Clement speaks of him elsewhere as 'our Pantaenus' and clearly regarded him with affec-tion.[5] He shared Pantaenus's interest in Indian wisdom, and is the first Christian to mention Buddhism. He especially praises Pantaenus's expositions of the Old and New Testaments because of their fidelity to the orthodox tradition received from the apostles. It appears that intelligence and orthodoxy were not commonly found together in second-century Alexandria. Whether Pan-taenus wrote anything is uncertain. Clement's long justification of his decision to put into writing his views on the higher reaches of doctrine at the beginning of the *Stromateis* proves that Pantaenus wrote nothing on these subjects, but does not exclude the possibility that he wrote tracts of an apologetic character addressed to pagan readers or to catechumens.[6] That the oral instruction he gave in lectures much influenced Clement is certain. But Bousset's erudite attempt to reconstruct some of his work on the hypothesis that Clement woodenly incorporated his lectures by scissors-and-paste methods is now agreed to have been a mistake[7]—one of those acts of folly that distinguished scholars are occasionally allowed to commit so that lesser mortals may continue undiscouraged with their studies.

The chief problem confronting Clement was a pastoral one. Alexandrian Christianity before his time is shrouded in mist, but what evidence there is suggests the powerful influence of gnostic thought and a tendency for the dividing line between heresy and orthodoxy to be less clearly drawn in Egypt than in Italy or Asia Minor.[8] Clement's work is an endeavour to mark this line more decisively, but without surrendering to the anti-intellectual reaction with which some believers were expressing their opposition to Gnosticism. As Clement saw, this reaction only made it all the easier for the Gnostics to steal the hearts of educated Christians repelled by the illiberalism and crudity of less instructed and thoughtful brethren.[9] Accordingly Clement has to meet the demand of thinking Christians for a more coherent account of their faith with the grounds for holding it, while at the same time steering them clear of heresy. He consistently refuses the choice between the Scylla of obscurantist orthodoxy and the Charybdis of heretical reinterpretations of the faith.

Clement's problems are largely the consequence of an internal tension within the Christian community. The orthodox are highly moral but not very intelligent. 'The so-called orthodox' (Clement observes) 'are like beasts which work out of fear; they do good works without knowing what they are doing.'[10] They especially distrust intellectuals. On the other side stand educated Christians deeply influenced and attracted by Valentinian Gnosticism with its generous fusion of Christianity, Platonism, and almost everything else as well.

The pagan Celsus had dismissed the Christians as either fools or knaves, consisting mainly of the former, but including a few intelligent people who could explain away crudities by forced allegory. The implication of Celsus's attack is always to represent Christianity as not just accidentally but fundamentally banausic, a religion the core of which is hostile to human values, however politely it may be dressed up, a farrago of pitiable and childish stuff aimed at entrapping illiterates, women, and slaves.[11] If, therefore, Celsus finds that educated people professedly believe it to be true, any concern that such people may show for literature, philosophy, and the classical tradition generally shows either that they do not take their religion seriously or that their apparently cultured interests are no more than an artificial trick to gain converts among the upper strata of society. What for Celsus is inconceivable is that any Christian should share a genuinely positive and sincere appreciation of human qualities.

On a rapid and superficial reading Clement might seem to lend a degree of confirmation and support to this thesis. The mannered allusions to philosophers and the innumerable quotations from poets seem to our modern taste greatly to overload his pages. He incorporates many snippets of verse which he demonstrably knows only from handbooks and anthologies rather than from first-hand acquaintance with the originals, since several of his quotations occur in the same form in other writers of the period. He seems to lose no opportunity of dragging in some curious piece of pedantry, almost as if his purpose were to empty the contents of a commonplace book. He gives an often entertaining commentary on high life at Alexandria with vivid descriptions of the absurd success symbols and bogus values. But parallels in Juvenal, Seneca, Petronius, and other writers remind us that to some of this writing there is a bookish flavour; it is in the literary tradition of ancient satire. Moreover, while Clement knows all the arts of rhetoric and the neatly turned arguments of the logicians, his Greek style is not pure by classical standards, as he himself well knows.[12] Does all this add up to the conclusion that we have to do with an artificial form assumed by Clement as a matter of missionary tactics and that Clement himself is not really at home in this literary and civilized world? Twice he justifies his literary and philosophical allusions (in face of potential Christian critics) by the example of St. Paul, whose declared method it was to be 'all things to all men that he might by any means save some'.[13] Are we to think of Clement as putting on a mere façade of urbanity but not really belonging in heart and mind to the educated, civilized strata of society which he seeks to win for the gospel?

Careful examination both of Clement and of his contemporaries leaves one in no doubt about the answer: Clement belongs to the world he is addressing.[14] If he uses anthologies of poets, so do many others of his type and class. If he drags in anecdotes and scraps of scholarly erudition in a faintly pedantic manner, we may find the same manner (exercised, it may be said, to infinitely more deadly effect) in writers of his time like Aelian, or in those donnish sages who converse over imaginary dinners in the pages of Athenaeus. Clement and they belong equally to an intellectual society where philosophical speculation is moving almost wholly within a framework of ideas laid down by Greek philosophers five or six hundred years previously, with the natural consequence that philosophy has become scholasticism and the instinct for scholarship has turned to an antiquarian passion for amassing facts. Again, the rhetorical expressions that irritate the modern reader were in the ancient context an asset. Judged by the standards of his pagan contemporaries Clement is very modest, and the luxuriance of his style is restrained. Content and meaning matter more to him than form and elegance. It is among his criticisms of classical humanism that it has tended to prize beauty at the expense of truth. It is beyond doubt that many of his quotations are borrowed from school anthologies and from collections anticipating the kind of thing John Stobaeus was to produce two or three centuries later. It can be shown that Stobaeus incorporated anthologies current centuries before his time. In an age when books were relatively costly, anthologies and excerpts were naturally popular, especially in education, and everyone used them. But it is indisputable that Clement has a first-hand familiarity with Homer and Plato, and highly probable that the same is true of his knowledge of Euripides and Menander. In general Clement faithfully mirrors the level of culture among men of letters in polite Alexandrian society at the end of the second century. Only he is aware (how could he help it?) of those who think Christianity only for the uneducated, and is therefore a little over-anxious to show how learned a Christian can be. There is a certain amount of name-dropping. But that fault is not a mark only of the *demi-monde*.

The truth which lends plausibility to the superficial view that he is a mere tactician is that, despite all his courteous and cultivated manner, he avows a sharply critical reserve towards the classical tradition of Greece. His reverence for the greatest and noblest achievements of Greek humanism is never unqualified. He loves Plato and Homer, but he does not read them on his knees. He does not think that either poetry or sculpture, when it is symbolic of pagan religion or morality, can be defended simply on the ground that its form is beautiful. Aesthetic beauty is for him not merely irrelevant but an actual snare if it expresses a corrupt moral attitude. Exquisite statues of Aphrodite may be fine work; but they may also express an attitude to sex that is wholly unacceptable, because they deify the creaturely and the this-worldly—they belong in essence to the seamy world of phallic religion.[15]

Clement stands on the same ground when he comes to survey the history of Greek religion.[16] The pre-Socratic philosophers, he says, did well to eliminate the immoral gods of myth who were in any event a set of frenzied womanizers for whom there is not a good word to be said. But they substituted for them materialistic principles. So far as the idea of God goes, it is no tremendous advance to have exchanged Poseidon for water. To take water or fire as ultimate principles in the universe is a failure to recognize the transcendent Creator and is in the last analysis comparable to the worship of stocks and stones or the Egyptian cult of sacred animals. When philosophers took the heavenly bodies to be gods this was at least some progress in the right direction; and Clement is prepared to accept the view (expressed in Deuteronomy iv. 19 and sanctioned by Philo) that the cult of the stars and planets may have been providentially allowed to heathen races as a stage in their emancipation from materialism and earthly idolatries.[17] Perhaps a similar defence might be offered for the deification of great men who became notable benefactors of humanity like Heracles, Asclepius, or Dionysus.[18] But as a whole, pagan cult is a potent evil force under demonic control.[19]

Clement agrees that he has no criticism of pagan religion and myth which is not taken from the philosophers and cannot be supported by quotations from Menander and the writers of the Comedy.[20] But even the philosophers have often failed to realize the transcendence of the Creator who must not be identified with the world or with any part of it. The Stoics, for example, are pantheists who believe that God is a spirit pervading all matter in this cosmic order. Aristotle identifies the supreme Father with the world soul, not perceiving the inconsistency of this with his doctrine that providence does not extend down to the sublunary sphere. Epicurus the hedonist even denies that the gods care at all for this world.[21] Of all the Greek philosophers far the best is Plato, who hit on the truth that God is one, transcendent and the first Cause of all things, an intuition that also comes to occasional expression in Euripides and other poets.[22] But the radical monotheism of Christianity is the full development of this recognition that God is greater than any of his works.

The intuition of divine truth Clement mentions on several occasions. The idea of God was implanted in man at Creation, breathed into Adam,[23] and there is no known race that does not possess the notion.[24] There is a spark of nobility in the soul, an upward inclination which is kindled by the divine Logos.[25] Faith is an intuitive inward testimony to the highest and best, a capacity for recognition.[26] Therefore the task of the Christian evangelist is to penetrate through the hindrances of evil tradition and idle opinion imposed by the binding force of custom and prejudice and to evoke that latent faith beneath, which is gratitude to our Creator—'a kind of rent we pay God for our dwelling here below'.[27] Man belongs to God and is made for the contemplation of God. This is what distinguishes him from the animals. It is that by virtue of which he is man. Therefore to hear the gospel of salvation in Christ and to refuse is to be false to the highest that you know, and to reject a categorical imperative which asks for obedience because you are what you are, namely the son of your Creator whose universal message is addressed to all men without distinction of race, class, or colour.[28]

Clement's account of the relation between Christianity and philosophy looks back to Philo on one side and to Justin on the other. He makes his own Philo's thesis that philosophy is a preparation for theology just as grammar prepares for more advanced study, and as geometry, astronomy, and music wean the mind from sense-perception and train it to conceive of non-empirical, abstract entities.[29] Justin he never mentions, but there can be little doubt that he had read his writings, even if he owes Justin less than Irenaeus does. Some of Justin's more obviously unsophisticated theses are dropped, but the essential pattern is recognizably the same. All wisdom is summed up in Christ, who is, as it were, the keystone of the arch of knowledge and its uniting principle.[30] Both the Old Testament and Greek philosophy are alike tutors to bring us to Christ and are both tributaries of the one great river of Christianity.[31] In Christ Clement possesses the full truth only partially apprehended by the different schools, each of which has discovered some element of the truth.[32] Accordingly he provides a theological justification to underpin his eclecticism, which is in practice the common blend of

Platonist metaphysics and Stoic ethics together with Aristotelian logic and terminology. But Clement does not know the philosophers only through eclectic handbooks arguing the harmony of Plato and Stoicism.[33] He has gone back to the sources for himself. And Aristotelian logic plays a much larger role for him than for Philo or for Justin, whose studies with his Peripatetic tutor were in any event too brief to be useful. Clement is well aware that logical questions are raised by Christian affirmations, especially by the nature of faith as an act of assent.[34]

Stoicism Clement criticizes on the same grounds as Justin: its pantheism and its rejection of belief in anything immaterial made it unacceptable to a Christian. But Clement owes much to Stoic ethics. Except for his censure of Stoic approval of suicide[35] and his criticism of the notion that mercy is an emotional weakness that the wise man will suppress,[36] Clement openly welcomes the body of Stoic moral teaching. The Christian, called to travel light in this world and to possess it as if he had it not, finds much in common with the Stoic for whom only inward moral virtue is necessary to happiness. Clement deliberately sets out to clothe his Christian ethic in the outward form of Stoic or Platonic teaching.[37] Eclectic philosophers before him had argued that the ethical ideal of Plato's *Theaetetus*, 'assimilation to God as far as possible', is in meaning identical with the Stoic ideal of 'life according to nature'.[38] It was no great step for Clement to identify both with the Christian doctrine that man must shape himself to correspond to his

Creator's purpose and that the measure of his depar-
ture from this is sin. Christ is the realization of the ideal
wise man of Stoic aspiration.[39] He is (as Justin said) the
'right reason' who brings control to our stormy passions.[40] Clement's account of Christian duties is indebted
not merely to the New Testament but to the whole Stoic
tradition of thought about the nature of moral obliga-
tions.[41] For pedagogic reasons the New Testament
writings speak of heavenly rewards for virtue and retri-
bution for vice. But Clement will not allow that there is
any mercenary element. The fear of hell and the hope
of heaven are only relevant for the motivation of very
inferior capacities.[42] The more advanced Christian
loves God and goodness for their own sake.[43] If he is
called to martyrdom, his motive is not selfish ambition
for a martyr's crown but integrity and love for
God.[44]

Clement's discussion of these delicate questions shows
a sensitivity to a common pagan objection which Justin
in his time had already begun to face but did not know
how to answer.[45] But Clement never loses his Christianity in a sea of Hellenism, even when he is treating of
popular ethics, where the pull towards a colourless and
undistinctive neutrality is powerful. He urges, for instance, that there is such a thing as a specifically Christian type of character, primarily modelled on the
example of the Lord himself, frugal, humble, unselfish,
generous, and cheerful. It is seen in a courtesy expressed
in the smallest details of life—in a man's gait when
walking, in his behaviour at meals, and in ordinary

social contacts—and yet it remains natural and unstrained.[46] He affirms, moreover, that the Christian ethic revealed by God is higher than the natural law which everyone takes for granted and which is implanted by creation in the souls of all men. Again, he maintains that the Christian ethic is more than advice and moral recommendation: it also speaks of grace and moral power.[47]

Clement's deepest instinct is to take the natural theology of the philosophers and all the correspondences between them and the Bible as the product of their own reflection as they used their God-given reason and contemplated the image of God within themselves.[48] Plato, Aristotle, and the Stoics were wise and clever men who found many truths out for themselves under the beneficent hand of God's providence. To deny that philosophy is God's gift is to deny providence and the image of God in Creation.[49] Clement rebuts the illiberal Christian appeal to St. Paul by the argument that, when the apostle told the Corinthians that the wisdom of this world is foolishness with God and the Colossians that they should 'beware of philosophy and vain deceit', he was warning them against bad philosophy like the Sceptical and Epicurean schools.[50] St. Paul's quotations from Aratus, Epimenides, and Menander prove that he had no superstitious fear of pagan literature.[51]

Beside the view that philosophy is born of the exercise of the divine gift of reason, Clement also believes that the Greeks found out many truths by plagiarizing the Old Testament.[52] And he is confronted by violently anti-gnostic Christians who think philosophy inspired by the devil.[53] The most that Clement is prepared to concede to them is that philosophy may have come down to men by transmission from the fallen angels of Genesis vi, who took wives of the daughters of men and disclosed to their women-folk priceless secrets.[54] It may have been stolen from heaven as Prometheus stole fire;[55] but is not fire beneficial? And if Satan does speak as a philosopher, he is transformed into an angel of light who speaks what is true. We must always judge truth by what is said, not by who says it.[56]

The plagiarism theme is developed by Clement more than by any other early Christian writer, and he follows Tatian rather than Justin in giving this thesis a polemical anti-Hellenic edge. Some of Clement's prickliness may be motivated by a desire to placate anti-philosophical Christians, for the theme is noticeably more prominent in the *Stromateis* than in the *Protrepticus*, where it occupies a modest place.[57] Justin had declared that Plato discovered in the Old Testament the doctrines of Creation, the Trinity, the Cross, and judgement hereafter. Clement considerably extends the list. For him the gospel according to Plato includes not only the Trinity, life after death,[58] and the createdness of the world as taught in the Timaeus, but also the devil who is the evil world soul of the *Laws*, the contrast of the intelligible and sensible worlds which Plato derived from the two accounts of Creation in Genesis (here Clement is following Philo), the idea of resurrection which Plato hints at in his myth of the resurrection of

Er the son of Armenius twelve days after his death, the Lord's day as the eighth day and so a symbol of the heavenly rest in the sphere of the fixed stars above the seven wandering planets, and Socrates' striking prophecy that a really righteous man will be so unacceptable to society that he will be scourged and 'after enduring every humiliation will be crucified'.[59]

For Clement as for Justin,[60] Socrates is a pattern of integrity vindicating Christian martyrs in their resistance to State tyranny;[61] and like Justin[62] Clement has high hopes for the salvation of Greek sages. God's saving purpose is not confined to his covenant with the Hebrews. His interest in the Gentile races did not begin only after the Incarnation.[63]

By a striking extension of the notion of the descent to Hades Clement explains a passage in the Shepherd of Hermas to mean that, just as the Lord preached to the Old Testament saints at his descent to Hades, so also the apostles at their deaths preached to the righteous Gentiles.[64]

Despite all Clement's censorious complaints against the plagiarism and theft of the Greek poets and philosophers, he is inwardly less critical of the classical tradition than Justin, whose expressions are so much more positive and welcoming than Clement's. In particular his acceptance of Platonism is more thoroughgoing, partly because he stands to a much greater degree than Justin under the direct influence of Philo[65] and therefore thinks of many Platonic doctrines as coming to him with Biblical authority to support them. Nevertheless, the heart of the matter for Clement always lies in the doctrine of the transcendent Creator upon whose will and providence the created order is dependent and with whom this world is in no sense identical. So he rejects the Stoic doctrine that goodness and virtue in God do not transcend the goodness and virtue of the perfect wise man and that virtue in both man and God is the same thing.[66] Likewise he rejects the Platonic doctrine that the sun, moon, and stars are invested with divine souls responsible for their perfectly orderly motion and are in fact gods. To Clement the stars are only powers which fulfil the command of their Creator and who control affairs on earth in obedience to his authority. Their prime duty is to mark the passage of time. Comets, thunderbolts, and other such celestial portents, however, are purely physical phenomena and must be given an entirely naturalistic explanation.[67]

The Platonic myth of Creation in the *Timaeus* he interprets as strictly parallel to Genesis, and the *Timaeus* could naturally be interpreted to support the view that the cosmos is created, not uncreated and eternal, though possessing permanence in dependence on the will of God.[68] But the question remains: is the matter of which this world is made something that existed 'prior to' the act of Creation? Three times Clement declares that the world is made 'out of nothing',[69] but in each case the phrase he employs is *ek me ontos*, not *ex ouk ontos*; that is to say, it is made not from that which is absolutely non-existent, but from relative non-being or unformed matter, so shadowy and vague that it cannot be said to have the status of 'being', which is imparted to it by the shaping hand of the Creator. Philo had used virtually the same language.[70] Justin is ambiguous but could be taken to suggest, like Tatian, that the Logos first created needed matter as raw material and then ordered it into cosmos. Athenagoras,[71] on the other hand, makes no attempt to interpret Creation as anything other than the ordering of pre-existent matter by the divine artist. Clement is evidently more sensitive than Athenagoras to the need for a doctrine that closes the door both to gnostic dualism and to monistic pantheism. For Irenaeus creation *ex nihilo* had seemed an essential affirmation to exclude Gnosticism,[72] and the point had been reinforced by the Gnostic Hermogenes whose central arguments were based upon the denial of this proposition.[73] Clement has read Irenaeus and at least knows about Hermogenes.[74] He absolutely denies the eternity of the cosmos or its creation 'in time'; for time was created with the Creation.[75] In relation to God 'before' and 'after' have no intelligible meaning. When Clement says that 'God was before becoming Creator',[76] he must therefore be understood to mean that the created order is not necessary to God. Photius[77] in the ninth century criticizes Clement on the ground that in his (lost) *Hypotyposes* or 'Outlines' Clement maintained the doctrine of 'timeless matter'. But in the *Paedagogus* he is explicit that 'nothing exists which God has not caused to exist'.[78] Photius's accusation is explicable if Clement regarded Creation as the imparting of form and qualities to matter in a state of relative non-being. Clement evidently thought that this sufficiently safeguarded divine transcendence.

Clement's attitude to the Platonic conception of the soul as having fallen from heaven to become imprisoned in matter is not perfectly clear. In one or two places the Platonic doctrine is implied, as when he says that 'Bodies are given to us as an outward covering for our entry into this common place of discipline',[79] but it is not quite explicit; and elsewhere he denies outright that 'the soul is sent down from heaven to a worse state'—God's way, he adds, is to raise us up, and heaven is our goal rather than a state from which we have descended.[80] The Platonic myth had too many awkward affinities with the gnostic position Clement is anxious to combat.[81] He can declare that the body is an obstacle to the soul's clarity of vision,[82] and that death snaps the chain binding the soul to the body;[83] but he refuses to concede that the body is in any sense evil. 'The soul is not good by nature, neither is the body evil.'[84] In the third book of the 'Miscellanies', where he undertakes a full-scale critique of the gnostic doctrine that the body and this material order of things are not the work of an omnipotent and beneficent Creator, Clement attacks the notion that sinfulness is a taint transmitted from Adam and Eve through sexual reproduction.[85] Moreover, a true understanding of the Incarnation absolutely excludes the idea that the physical condition of man can be evil.[86] But Clement grants that to be created is to be involved in transitoriness and finitude.[87] If he accepts the pre-existence of souls, he does not allow uncreatedness.

Immortality is a gift of salvation in Christ, not an inherent possession of the soul.[88] There is a gulf between the Creator and the creature, and it is a fundamental criticism of the gnostic doctrine that the elect are of one substance with God that it obliterates this distinction.[89]

Photius charges Clement with teaching the transmigration of souls. The truth may be that he discussed the doctrine without making clear his attitude towards it, for the *Stromateis* do not bear out Photius's contention.[90] He once observes that if a Christian eats no meat it will not be because he accepts the Pythagorean myth of transmigration into animals.[91] He rejects without hesitation the Stoic doctrine of world-cycles, and regards the Stoic belief that at determined periods the cosmos is transmuted into fire as a misunderstanding of Bible teaching about the fire of God's judgement. Clement's mind is so strongly anti-determinist that it is improbable that he ever accepted the fatalistic conception of transmigration.[92]

Clement never mentions Celsus and perhaps had never read or even heard of his work. Yet there are several points where Clement may have had either Celsus or some comparable critic in mind. The nerve-centre of the Platonist onslaught in Celsus lies in his denial of freedom in God and his insistence that the immutability of the cosmos and the immutability of God are correlative. A universal providence exercises a general benevolence that excludes all particularity, and the concept of a unique Incarnation is unthinkable. Clement implicitly answers the objection by setting the Incarnation within the universal context of divine purpose and human destiny. The Incarnation is not asserted as self-explanatory taken in isolation, but is seen as a nodal point in the total development of the divine intention for the human race. Clement brings everything under the single principle of the education of mankind, a conception of which the seeds are already found in St. Paul in the epistles to the Galatians and to the Ephesians, and which is especially worked out by Irenaeus in dealing with the difficulties of the Old Testament. Admittedly Clement has not a real 'theology of history' in the sense that Irenaeus has. He does not think of progressive education disclosing new truth. For him truth is eternal and unchanging, and the gospel is a republication of the primordial revelation given by God to the earliest man, but corrupted into polytheism. Philosophy, with its acids of scepticism as well as its high morality, was given by God to the Greeks as a remedy against sin, just as the Law was given to the Jews.[93] The Biblical story is the narrative of God educating humanity back to himself, sometimes by severity as in the Flood and other miracles,[94] but throughout acting with a purpose of love which has its pre-eminent manifestation in the incarnate Lord. The Incarnation is therefore a special case of divine immanence[95] and presupposes that providence is not so confined to generalities that particular care for the enfeebled soul of humanity is excluded.[96] The crucifixion shows how God deals with evil, not preventing it from occurring but bringing good out of evil.[97]

The true being of the incarnate Lord was not manifest to all, but only to those with the spiritual capacity to receive the revelation.[98] It was no play-acting, but a genuine taking of flesh[99] by the mediating Logos, the high priest who is not ashamed to call us brethren.[100] He ate and drank, admittedly (Clement concedes) not because food was necessary to the Lord whose body was sustained by divine power, but to prevent heretical notions getting about.[101] Clement may be forgiven if he has no fully developed answer to the question, put by Celsus,[102] how the divinity of Christ is tenable by a monotheist. He thinks of the divine Logos as the Father's will and energy[103] (not, however, as the expression of God's latent reason, since this way of thinking is almost gnostic);[104] the Logos is the Father's servant in relation to the world,[105] and this ministerial role evidently safeguards monotheism for Clement as much as the unity of Son and Father, which he likewise stresses. He rejects the simple solution of the Adoptionists with their doctrine that Jesus was so good a man that he was elevated by the Father to divine status.[106]

Some of Clement's most instructive writing concerns the nature of faith, and his discussions in the second and fifth books of the 'Miscellanies' may be described as the first Christian essay in aid of a grammar of assent. Clement seeks to relate the act of faith to the epistemological debates of the philosophical schools about the nature of proof and the ground of assent. This question was being thrust upon Clement from three different sides and, although he was not able to work out a completely consistent position with precise terminology on the basis of which he could confront all adversaries, at least his efforts have the high interest of a pioneer attempt. His main concern is to meet the pagan critic who scorns faith as an unreasoning opinion formed without proper consideration—the argument, of course, by which Lucian had sought to discredit all philosophical systems (above, pp. 20 f.). Clement replies, first, that all argument has to take something for granted, and faith in religious knowledge is analogous to those initial postulates which make subsequent discussion possible.[107] No first principles can be proved, and it is an error to demand demonstration of them. Secondly, nothing whatever can be known unless the intellect is propelled in a certain direction by the will. So faith is a choice of the will and becomes the basis not only of knowledge but also of ethical action.[108] Thirdly, faith is assent to the authority of God, a recognition of his word spoken through inspired prophets.[109] To the authority of divine love it is reasonable to give assent, for God is worthy of trust. Yet faith in this authority is not blind submission, but a freely given co-operation, in which the relationship is like that of a father and his son or a shepherd with his sheep. The submission of faith is not grovelling servility but spontaneous love and gratitude.[110]

Clement's remarks here show a noteworthy sensitivity to the problems of authority in religion. He once observes in another context that the meek pronounced blessed by Christ are those who are meek by deliberate choice, not those who cannot help being meek because it is their nature to be submissive.[111]

The second front on which Clement has to fight in dealing with the nature of faith is that of the Gnostics who disparage faith as an inferior grade for ordinary Church members, while their own initiates are a spiritual aristocracy, rejoicing in their divine election and in the possession of *gnosis*, by which is meant a higher non-rational knowledge imparted by revelation and so esoteric. Against the Gnostics Clement maintains the perfection of baptism and the sufficiency of faith for salvation.[112] There is no stage in the Christian's progress where he leaves faith behind, since he is always in the position of a child trusting his father in simplicity and sincerity (a leading theme in the first book of the *Paedagogus*).

But at this point Clement has immediately to face his third group of critics, the simple believers. They insist on the all-sufficiency of faith; but by faith they mean an unreflective acceptance of what is given to them on authority.[113] Clement must therefore deny the gnostic assertion that faith and knowledge represent radically distinct and pre-determined grades of religious apprehension, yet without surrendering to the view that there is no place for advance in theological and spiritual comprehension in the course of the Christian life. 'All the elect are good', he once remarks in a sentence that strikingly anticipates George Orwell, 'but some are more elect than others'.[114] For mature and thoughtful Christians will seek for profounder understanding than that contained in the simple outlines of catechetical instruction.[115] They will strive to penetrate beyond the letter of scripture to its inward spiritual meaning,[116] just as they aspire to pass beyond petitions for material benefits to prayer for moral goodness and for progress in spiritual insight and in contemplation.[117] This is the way of 'the true gnostic', a ladder of divine ascent from faith and knowledge up to the beatific vision which lies beyond this life, a way of prayer in which the contemplative passes beyond verbal prayer to a purely mental act from which all awareness of the phenomenal world of sense has been set aside. Learning and the study of books are not necessary to salvation; one can be a very good Christian and be unable to read or write. But this does not mean that advanced theological study is superfluous or that there are not higher levels of the spiritual life than those attained by neophytes.

The 'true gnostic' is able to give a coherent and reasoned account of what is known in faith only in summary and general form.[118] His intellectual grasp, however, is morally conditioned. Insight is given to the pure in heart. It is a gift of grace as the Father draws to himself the one who lives a pure life.[119] This does not do away with free will, for it is the human part to co-operate with grace in a free personal relationship.[120] Grace is not automatic. It is a heretical error to say that redemption is a natural and inevitable process, since this eliminates freedom from both God and man.[121] It loses the paradoxical character of divine love and mercy. To Clement it is the crowning demonstration of the goodness of God that he cares for sinful men estranged from him.[122] But God uses persuasion, never force.[123] His punishments are always an expression of his love and righteousness.[124] The fire of his judgement hereafter is not devouring but discerning, purging away all defilement from our souls in a purification which scripture calls baptism by fire,[125] so that we may be made fit to be near the Lord in the *apocatastasis* or final restoration.[126] For Christ wills to save all. By discipline the soul becomes indefectibly bound to the divine love, as habit becomes nature.[127] The knowledge of God and everlasting salvation are in truth identical; but if the 'true gnostic' were forced to choose between them, he would unhesitatingly choose the former, preferring dynamic advance to static possession.[128] Ever higher, onward and upward he ascends, cleaving the heavens, passing every angelic and spiritual power to attain the radiancy of the vision of God 'face to face'.[129] Salvation is 'deification', union with God, symbolized by Moses in the darkness on Sinai[130] or the high priest entering the holy of holies.[131] Philo had used the same language.[132] Only Clement does not think this union with God is to be attained during this life.

Clement knows some who find Biblical language about God altogether too anthropomorphic. He stresses that its character is symbolic and equivocal. The Father is not only beyond this world of space and time, but beyond all comprehension and description by human wisdom. Words cannot express and the mind cannot grasp what God is. That is why revelation is through the Son, who is the Alpha and Omega and the limit of our knowledge; the supreme Father transcends the possibility of our understanding.[133] We can form some notion of what he is not by the method of negation, a process of dialectical regress analogous to that used when we think of a geometrical point. To conceive of a point we must take away all magnitude, all physical qualities, all dimensions of height, breadth, and length, until nothing is left but position. Abstract position and only the idea of unity remains. We must follow this road to the knowledge of God, stripping off all corporeal, and indeed incorporeal, notions, at the last casting ourselves into the greatness of Christ for the final ascent to the Unconditioned.[134] Lest we think of God as the first in a series of numbers, we must affirm (as Philo had done) that God is 'beyond the One and beyond the Monad'.[135]

The *via negativa* brings Clement near to the point of an agnosticism that sees all utterance about God as symbol that may be subjectively useful to the user but may also have no objective correspondence with reality. This is not Clement's intention. He does not forget to emphasize that 'the greatness of Christ' is that on which the believer trusts for the knowledge of God. He is in part motivated by an anxiety to vindicate revelation: God, he says, is so utterly transcendent that we can know nothing at all about him except by grace.[136] It is the Irenaean (and Philonic) principle that through God alone can God be known, but expressed in the terminology of contemporary Platonic and Pythagorean philosophy. There are close analogies to Clement's language in Philo who obviously taught him much, though there are also notable differences. For Philo uses ecstatic and lyrical terms to describe the 'sober intoxication' of the soul,[137] goaded to 'corybantic frenzy' by the vision of God, overcoming the multiplicity of experience in a unitive knowledge of the ground of being. The springs of this terminology lie in the three Platonic dialogues, *Ion*, *Phaedrus*, and *Symposium*. It is noteworthy that neither Justin nor Clement uses it, though Clement is happy to use Dionysiac imagery in the *Protrepticus* to describe the Logos as a hierophant inviting mankind to share in his mysteries.[138]

Clement in practice qualifies his impersonalist language very profoundly. The content of his doctrine of God is in fact the divine love and goodness manifest in Christ and going back to the Creation. That man is made in the image of God means that man has the capacity to know his Maker; it does not mean a monistic mysticism in which the soul and God are ultimately an undifferentiated identity.

So the basic principle to which Clement repeatedly appeals is God's Creation. Because the Creator is the transcendent God, not to be identified with the world, Christians must reject all pagan worship of the creature, all philosophical pantheism, and any doctrine that material principles are ultimate. Because God is self-sufficient and does not need the created order to be himself, the world is contingent and is not coeternal with God. It is created and therefore moves to an end. Because the material world is the Creator's good gift to be received with thanksgiving, there can be no compromise with the gnostic dualism which makes matter

wholly alien and hostile to the supreme God. Because
the Creator's nature is goodness and love, his Creation
is an experiment in freedom in which he allows that
which derives its being from his will to be other than
himself and to turn away from him. There is no room
for gnostic determinism any more than for pagan fatalism and astrology. Because the Creator has implanted
his image in every man, though it has become obscured,
yet the intuitions of God in all men and the reasonings
of philosophy are God-given and must be given a positive value by Christians. Just as human freedom and
divine grace co-operate, so also reason and revelation
are complementary.

The doctrine of Creation is the foundation of Clement's ethic. In *Stromateis* III he attacks the gnostic
view that the material world is evil, especially as expressed in the heretics' attitude to marriage. The gnostic
sects divide into two groups: those which reject marriage
as incompatible with the spiritual life or those which
regard the body as indifferent and end in the indulgence
of wild sexual licence. The Antinomians especially appealed to St. Paul to justify their doctrine that for the
sons of the kingdom there can be no restraint or fear and
that the sole ethical principle is love. They defended
themselves with the plea that experience is self-justify-
ing, and even exploited the *Symposium* of Plato to provide an idealization of erotic ecstasy as a mystical
communion with God.[139] Clement replies by reasserting
the rightful place of law and rules in the moral life, and
by the argument that we are to accept this life from our

Creator with gratitude and with respect for his intentions.[140]

The ascetic Gnostics likewise appealed to St. Paul and Plato—to 1 Corinthians vii and to the Platonic myth of the soul's fall into matter. Clement denies the validity of the gnostic appeal, though he has to concede that the Platonic world-view has certain affinities with the gnostic position. God made the material world. There is nothing to be ashamed of in the body. Marriage is ordained of God who made man male and female and knew what he was about when he did so.[141] To beget children is not merely a duty to society but also co-operating with the Creator.[142] While some may be called to celibacy as part of their vocation to a higher spiritual life, it is wrong to regard celibacy as inherently nearer to God than the married state,[143] as if sexual intercourse involved a ceremonial or moral defilement.[144] In fact, the married man has greater opportunities for sanctification than the celibate, since he faces the daily exasperations that come to him from his wife, his children, and his household responsibilities.[145] Among the apostles, moreover, there were married men like St. Peter, and St. Paul addresses his wife in Philippians iv as 'thou true yokefellow'. He would have taken his wife about with him, like St. Peter, if his strenuous missionary adventures (perhaps Clement was thinking of the basket in which the apostle escaped from Damascus) had not made that impossible.[146] But Clement attacks mere self-indulgence. Conjugal relations are for the natural purpose of begetting children,[147] and married love requires much restraint and respect. Excess and satiety kill love.[148]

Clement's sex ethic owes much of its inspiration to Stoic moralists like Musonius Rufus,[149] who likewise combines a vindication of marriage with an austere condemnation of self-indulgence and of unnatural practices like abortion and homosexual vice. Clement's opposition to the fanaticism of gnostic asceticism, which was often marked (as in Marcion's case) by a pathological recoil from sexuality, does not lead him into a naturalistic hedonism.

Again, wine is a good gift of God to be received with thanksgiving.[150] Drunkenness is disgusting and wrong, but the modest consumption of a glass of wine at an occasional dinner-party,[151] especially by older people whose blood is cooler, is not only permissible but is sanctioned by the authority of Plato and by the Lord in the miracle of Cana, while St. Paul exhorted Timothy to take a little wine for his stomach's sake. To a teetotalism which would impose prohibition on all as a fundamental moral principle Clement is absolutely opposed (the more so because he felt the force of the prohibitionist argument), and he makes no concessions to a sectarian demand that water rather than wine should be used in the Eucharist. But the very fact that the Lord's supper precludes such fanatical puritanism means that the glass of wine which the Christian drinks when he is out to dinner must be to him a reminder of the sacrament of our redemption, and he will therefore drink with reverence. And for individual abstinence as opposed to universal prohibition Clement has profound respect. In practice the direction of Clement's recommendations for conduct is always in the direction of strictness. His ideal is simplicity without ostentation or luxury, limited to what is necessary for life and health, and eschewing indulgence in finery and opulence.

A special problem of pastoral care was created for Clement by the gospel narrative concerning the rich young ruler to whom the Lord said, 'if thou wouldest be perfect, sell that thou hast. . . .' The passage was felt as a difficulty by the upper-class converts of Alexandria to whom Clement especially addressed himself. Clement treats the text not as a legal demand but as God's highest purpose for those who desire to serve him to the uttermost. It is not possession of wealth, but the use of it and the attitude towards it that count in God's sight. Clement proceeds to lay down a most rigorous programme of disciplined, charitable almsgiving. Here again, the Stoics had helped to point the way for him: his treatment of the subject is closely analogous to that of Seneca.[152]

Throughout the discussion of morality and polite etiquette in the *Paedagogus* the same story appears. The Christian is to have as one who has not. He is to accept the world as the good gift of God, but to remain detached from it as a pilgrim and sojourner.[153] Much that Clement protests to be lawful he does not regard as expedient. Stage plays do not fall within his range of what is permissible, though he is aware that a case is put for them by some Christians on the ground that they are a healthy recreation.[154] A Christian woman is to be restrained in dress, which does not mean that she may be slovenly or dowdy, and is only allowed cosmetics if she is married to a pagan husband—in which case she may need them to hold him.[155] Dyed or false hair is to be deplored: Clement's ladies were evidently given to a fashion that required false hair, since he has to use the desperate (and characteristically absurd) argument that it might render the validity of confirmation doubtful.[156] Baths are a luxury to be treated with stern moderation.[157] There is to be no compromise with the world in eating meat previously sacrificed to idols[158] or in military service;[159] and the Christian will avoid the use of oaths.[160] Physical exercise and sport are good in moderation for the sake of physical health, but should not be pursued for personal pride. Fishing seems to Clement a sport appropriate for a Christian gentleman; it has apostolic precedent.[161] There is to be no compromise with the eroticism of pagan society, and therefore the Christian will avoid dance music that provokes sensuality;[162] and in choosing a signet ring he will have a seal fitting for his Christian profession like a dove, or a fish, or a ship, or a lyre (like Polycrates of Samos in the familiar story of Herodotus) or an anchor (like king Seleucus I), not symbols suggesting idolatry or erotic passion or drink.[163]

To the objection that he is eliminating all distinction and fastidiousness from life[164] Clement replies that moral goodness is more than elegance and that external ornaments are nothing. *Sic transit gloria mundi*. To the objection that his moral demands are far too strict and that no one could reasonably maintain so exalted a standard, Clement yields no ground. He does not apologize at any point, and is not prepared to tell his disciples that they need not take him too seriously.[165] Let them remember, however, that the Church is a school for sinners, a *didaskaleion*,[166] that there is room for penitence within the Christian life,[167] and that the acquisition of perfection is no sudden thing but a gradual shaping of the character by divine grace.[168] All that is required is that we follow without reservation the highest we have been able to see.

It will be evident that nothing could be more mistaken than to think of Clement as a comfortable and worldly figure. He loves to quote 'God gives us all things richly to enjoy', but this never means for him an easygoing laxity. 'Nothing is more destructive to the soul than continual pleasure.'[169] 'Those who continually go to the limit of what is lawful quickly lapse into what is unlawful.'[170] The Christian life is a ceaseless conflict with the downward pull of the passions, and the disciple must learn to rise through the 'moderation' of Aristotelian ethics to achieve the passionlessness (*apatheia*) of the Stoics,[171] a calm tranquillity of silent worship which is a life of continual joy in prayer like that of the angels.[172] Side by side, therefore, with Clement's instruction for his educated and even wealthy converts living in the world, married, active in commerce, perhaps entrusted with positions of civil authority, there are elements that point forward towards the spirituality of the monks, withdrawn from society and devoted to contemplation in solitariness. In this spiritual ideal Clement owes a substantial debt to Platonic and especially Neopythagorean teaching, with self-discipline as a preparation for individual immortality, an ethic of celibacy and vegetarianism, and a quietist attitude to 'secular' society. Clement also anticipates later monastic practice by developing the idea of the 'true gnostic' as a spiritual director, mediating truth, like an inspired prophet, to less advanced disciples, for whom he intercedes, filling the place left vacant by the apostles and giving an authoritative interpretation of holy scripture.[173]

Clement is hellenized to the core of his being, yet unreserved in his adhesion to the Church in the sense of being wholly opposed to Gnosticism and bound to the authority of scripture as inspired revelation by which alone he has certitude concerning God's will and purpose. It is true that he is far removed from the popular theology that a man like Justin Martyr takes for granted. He has no place for the primitive eschatology, and stands in this respect under the direct influence of St. John and the epistle to the Ephesians, and much, of course, under that of philosophical idealism. The Church itself and the sacraments are for Clement spiritual symbols valuable for the evocation of individual spiritual life. He writes as a man of scholarship and urbane culture who has found in Christianity the best thing life has to give and a religious vantage point from which he can look out upon the contemporary intellectual scene. Like Justin and Tertullian he is a lay teacher of philosophy (which for him means Christian philosophy) not a formally accredited and ordained priest. But there does not appear to have been tension between him and the Alexandrian clergy. Clement is a trusted figure of whom the Alexandrian church is proud. His entire character and personal achievement constitute in themselves an answer to Celsus's thesis that between Christianity and the Hellenic tradition there can be no reconciliation.

THE ILLIBERAL HUMANIST

ORIGEN is not a figure it is easy to see in accurate perspective. This difficulty is not caused merely by the massive dimensions of his work, nor because he is especially obscure, nor even because we do not possess the full original text of his most controversial treatise. The primary reason is perhaps that some of his most characteristic themes, warmly debated during his lifetime and a stone of stumbling to many in the three hundred years following his death, have remained to this day permanently troubling questions in the history of Christian thought. It is notoriously difficult to handle him with that critical spirit which requires sympathy and impartiality from the historian.

Clement was a convert from paganism. Origen's parents were, or at least became, Christians. We have two rival and contradictory accounts of Origen's family, one from Eusebius of Caesarea and one from the inveterate enemy of Christianity, Porphyry.[1] According to Porphyry Origen was born and educated as a pagan. Eusebius says his parents were Christians and that his father, Leonides, was martyred in the persecution of 202 at Alexandria. As Eusebius is able to quote a sentence from a letter from Origen to his father exhorting

him to stand firm in his hour of trial,[2] it may reasonably
be assumed that Eusebius was at least correct in thinking they became Christians, though it is possible that
they were not so at the time of Origen's birth. A large
portion of what we know of Origen's life comes from the
sixth book of Eusebius's *Ecclesiastical History*. This is not
only a high climax of Eusebius's work, but also dependent on a 'Defence of Origen' compiled by Eusebius
and his teacher, the martyr Pamphilus. (One of the six
books of this work survives in a. Latin translation by
Rufinus.) For Eusebius Origen is a supreme saint and
hero, the realization of his highest intellectual and
spiritual ideals. The life of Origen is written in a hagiographical tone, and freely uses oral tradition and gossip.
But Eusebius had gone to the trouble of assembling
over 100 of Origen's letters,[3] several of which he quotes.
Whenever Eusebius is using documents contemporary
with the events he is describing, his authority is first-
class. Whenever he depends on no more than hearsay
and oral tradition, his authority is not higher than that
of any reasonably conscientious gossip-writer. As he is
careful to say when he has documentary authority, it is
not hard to distinguish which parts of his life of Origen
are authoritative and which should be treated with
caution and reserve. For example, the notorious story
that Origen castrated himself so as to be able to work
more freely in instructing female catechumens[4] may
perhaps be true, since such occasional acts of extreme
enthusiasm are attested in this period of the early
Church.[5] But the story is not among those for which

Eusebius quotes contemporary documents. He depends on an unwritten tradition. Near the end of his life Origen wrote a commentary on St. Matthew, in which he deplores the fanaticism of exegetes who have interpreted Matthew xix. 12 literally.[6] Epiphanius in the fourth century records the existence of a rival tradition that Origen's amazing chastity was achieved by drugs rather than by a knife.[7] Possibly both stories were generated by no more than malicious gossip. It is certain, at least, that the extreme self-denial of Origen's life as a young teacher provoked much notice and envious comment, sharpened by the stringency of his own outspoken criticisms of the worldly compromises of clergy and laity. He lived on the minimum of sleep and food. Taking seriously the gospel counsel of poverty, he sold his books of literature and philosophy.

According to Porphyry Origen attended the lectures of Ammonius Saccas,[8] an esoteric eclectic Platonist, with whom some eleven years later Plotinus was to study. Ammonius is a figure largely lost in the mist. The prime source of information about him is Porphyry, who says that Ammonius was the child of Christian parents but abandoned Christianity for the old religion. Ammonius's esoteric teaching moved Plotinus to desire Persian and Indian wisdom (which may suggest some sort of Neopythagoreanism, in spirit akin to that of Numenius of Apamea a generation before him). In his *Life of Plotinus* Porphyry mentions an Origen as one of Plotinus's fellow-students under Ammonius. It is so difficult to reconcile Porphyry's statements about this Origen with what is known of the Christian Origen that almost all scholars recognize the existence of two Origens. The Origen of the *Life of Plotinus* is treated by Porphyry as wholly one of the Neoplatonic circle. It is this Origen who is quoted by later pagan writers such as Eunapius, Hierocles, and especially Proclus, none of whom betrays the least awareness that these quotations might have come from a Christian writer.[9] What the Christian Origen learnt from Ammonius is beyond identification. It is at least certain that his writings display a masterly knowledge of the debates of the Greek philosophical schools and first-hand acquaintance with the works of Plato and Chrysippus.

As a teacher Origen began by giving instruction in grammar (by which he earned enough to keep his bereaved family) and in catechetical teaching. Eusebius says that he began work as a catechist, during the persecution when the normal official instruction (under the bishop) had ceased, at the request of individual converts who desired to be prepared for baptism. Whether this was the beginning of tension with Demetrius, the bishop of Alexandria, can only be a matter for conjecture. Demetrius gave Origen his authorization when the storms of persecution died down. But in Origen's act there may have been some implicit criticism of the fact that the bishop's official teaching was not being given for a time. To a stern ascetic, episcopal 'discretion' might well appear to be moral compromise. The story of his subsequent relations with Demetrius is one of mounting tension and distrust.

Origen divided his pupils into two categories, of which he took the more advanced, while the more elementary teaching was entrusted to Heraclas, a Christian whom he had first met at the lectures of Ammonius Saccas and who was later to become bishop of Alexandria. During this period (from about 212) he learnt Hebrew from a Christian Jew and compiled his Hexapla, a vast synopsis of the various versions of the Old Testament: first the Hebrew, and a transliteration of the Hebrew into Greek characters, the purpose of which is not perfectly clear (the most likely explanation is that some churches had preserved the old synagogue practice of having the Old Testament read in Hebrew even if they did not understand it); then the standard Septuagint version, generally used by the Greek churches and regarded as authoritative, with the rival translations of Aquila, Symmachus, and Theodotion, while, for the Psalms, two additional translations were added, one of which Origen had discovered himself in a jar in the Jordan valley, presumably in some collection of manuscripts very like that found at Qumran. Any words in the Septuagint differing from the Hebrew he marked with an obelus, indicating doubt about their authority, while supplements to the Septuagintal text, marked with asterisks, were added from the version of Theodotion. The Hexapla was designed for use. Origen had learnt from disputations with Rabbis that it was of no value to appeal to books or to a text of which they did not recognize the authority. During the third century the different churches were becoming much more aware than they had been earlier of divergent customs among themselves in accepting certain books in their lectionary. The majority view regarded the Septuagint as authoritative and inspired, but because of the lack of complete unanimity among churches and because of the continual debate with the synagogue only the Hebrew canon could be regarded as possessing wholly certain authority. The silent implication of Origen's view is that it is not safe to appeal only to the Septuagint to establish a point of fundamental doctrine. It is a consequence of the explicit deduction drawn from this view by Jerome that in English Bibles the overplus of the Septuagint canon over the Hebrew is separately printed, under the thoroughly misleading title 'Apocrypha'.

The text and exposition of the Bible stand at the very centre of Origen's work. The main bulk of his writings consists of sermons preached to congregations (mainly at Caesarea in Palestine whither he migrated in 230–1 after his relations with Bishop Demetrius had reached breaking-point), commentaries giving a full-scale exposition of immense detail, and 'scholia' or brief notes on particular points in certain books (though, as none of the scholia has been preserved directly by the manuscript tradition, their precise character is none too clear and one can argue only from analogy). One of his early works was entitled *Stromateis*, but only a few fragments survive. Among other topics Origen sought in this work to translate into Platonic language some basic New Testament ideas like 'eternal life' and to show the harmony of Jesus and Plato.[10] The endeavour suggests that Origen's *Stromateis* had at least something in common with Clement's, and perhaps he thought of himself as continuing where Clement's work had been left unfinished. On several occasions Clement announced his intention of discussing 'first principles' (*archai*) and the creation of the world,[11] but his intention was never realized. Origen may have wished to fill the gap when he wrote his own fateful treatise 'On First Principles', consisting in the main of an elaborate refutation of gnostic dualism and determinism directed against Marcion, Valentine, and Basilides, and a pioneer attempt to lay down rules for the right interpretation of the Bible.[12] The undertaking necessitated a general statement on the fundamentals of Christian doctrine such as Clement had never produced, but it is wrong to think of Origen's 'First Principles' as a systematic *Summa Theologica*. It is systematic in the sense that Origen opposes to the gnostic theology a coherent and self-consistent view of Christian doctrine, but its essential character is exploratory rather than dogmatic. 'Soundings' might have been an appropriate title for it. On several occasions he reviews various possible opinions and leaves to the reader a decision about the correct view. And although the first four words are a reminiscence of Plato's *Gorgias*, the work is not intended to be a synthesis of Christianity and Platonism. Its primary intention is anti-gnostic polemic; and as in the fourth gospel or the epistle to the Colossians this attack partly takes the form of silent concession, endeavouring to take over any of the positive values of the system of thought Origen is opposing and incorporating them within an orthodox scheme.

A similar need to oppose Valentinian Gnosticism gave Origen the initial impetus to write his commentary on St. John, which became a vast work of thirty-two tomes, of which the medieval scribes only had the courage and energy to transcribe the greater part of nine. This was dedicated to his patron Ambrose, whom he had converted from Valentinianism, and who regretted that, while there existed learned heretical commentaries like that of Heracleon, nothing comparable existed from the orthodox side. The commentary is remarkable for some speculative flights, no doubt designed to show Ambrose that orthodoxy is not duller than heresy. Clement of Alexandria had spoken of St. John as a 'spiritual gospel' in contrast to the three Synoptists who recorded the outward facts.[13] Origen likewise sees that the fourth evangelist's divergences from the synoptic tradition are bound up with theological rather than historical considerations: it was the purpose of the evangelists to give the truth, where possible, at once spiritually and corporeally (or outwardly), but where this was impossible, to prefer the spirit to the body, 'the true spiritual meaning being often preserved, as one might say, in the corporeal falsehood'.[14] None can understand the profundity of the gospel unless he has first, with the author, leant on Jesus's breast.[15] Accordingly, Origen's exposition is in search of a spiritual meaning which is not heretical and yet goes deeper than the surface meaning apparent to ordinary Church readers.

Because much of his work consists of an exposition of scripture Origen's writings bear a closer kinship than Clement's to the great allegorical commentary of Philo on the Pentateuch. 'Philo's commentaries on the Mosaic Law' (he once remarks) 'are read by judicious and intelligent men'.[16] Allegorical principles were securely guaranteed by the authority of St. Paul treating as allegory the story of Hagar and Sarah (Galatians iv) or by his declaration in 2 Corinthians iii that the spirit gives life, while the letter kills. Philo had found in the Pentateuch a mass of Greek philosophy, psychology, ethics, and natural science. Origen takes the method but modifies the results, fusing Philonic allegory with the typological methods of Justin and Irenaeus, by which the Old Testament contained not moralizing generalities expressed in the obscure form of history, geography, or law, but specific foreshadowings of the concrete redemptive acts of God in Christ. Origen takes as axiomatic Philo's principle that nothing unworthy of God can be intended by the inspired writers, and that passages in the Old Testament speaking of God as changing his mind or as angry and threatening prove only that in mercy God accommodates himself to the level of mean capacities which can only think in such picture language. There is in fact a scale of apprehension, and higher minds perceive truths in the Bible that are obscure to inferior understandings. Most texts in scripture have a literal and historical meaning, but that this is not the only or primary meaning is shown by certain passages which are literally impossible, placed there by providence as evidence to guide the reader to the spiritual truth. The allegorical meaning may not be simple; and two, three, or even four concurrent levels of meaning may be found in some passages. The Song of Songs, for example, has two spiritual interpretations, one concerning Christ and the Church, another concerning the union of the Logos with the individual soul. Origen sometimes justifies this doctrine of concurrent meanings by taking the human analogy of body and soul which Philo and Clement had used before him, only modifying it in accordance with the Pauline division of man into three parts—body, soul, and spirit.[17]

Because revelation is an accommodation to differing levels and capacities, Christian doctrine is capable of varying statements. The higher flights are not only not understood by inferior minds but are actually suspected of being heretical, and therefore have to be treated as esoteric and mysterious. A full account it is hardly safe to commit to writing. But Origen's constant endeavour is to bring the existence of higher insights to the attention of inferior capacities and to provoke them to advance in the spiritual and moral life, so that in time they too may come to understand matters now beyond their range. Literalist exegesis of the Bible produces bizarre crudities, and simple readers of the Old Testament believe things of God that would not be credible of the most savage and unjust men.[18] The diversity of mental capacity in the Church is so great as to impose intense difficulties upon a Christian teacher. He must speak without upsetting the simple, yet without starving the more intelligent.[19] Origen suggests that many Christian teachers are failing in their duty to the sharper minds in their congregations. Probably, he thinks, private instruction is best suited for them—just as the Lord himself spoke in pictures and parables to 'those without', while within the house he explained everything privately to the disciples.[20] Likewise there is the example of St. Paul, who had indeed a higher wisdom expounded to the perfect, but was prepared to accommodate himself to the carnal Corinthians, capable only of milk, not of solid meat. To them the apostle determined to know nothing but the crucified Christ of humiliation; they were not yet worthy of the *theologia gloriae*.[21]

In his commentary on St. John Origen collects from scripture the titles of Christ.[22] It is a consequence of the redeeming grace of Christ that he is all things to all, to each according to his need, and is therefore variously apprehended by believers. We begin by knowing Jesus as redeemer and physician, curing us of sin and passion, but we are to advance to know him under other forms and titles, as life, light, truth, and wisdom. The Logos as the mediator of God's revelation is like the steps leading up to the holy of holies in the Temple,[23] and we are gradually to ascend until we know him, not as he wills to be initially for our sakes, but as he truly is in himself. This is for Origen the principle of the Incarnation, and he finds it powerfully reinforced by the symbolic narra-

tive of the transfiguration: to the inner circle of disciples
on the mount Christ's true glory is disclosed, but to
those on the plain his appearance may betray nothing
of the mystery of his being. So John the Baptist was able
to tell the Pharisees that 'there stands one among you
whom you do not recognize' (John i. 27). Although
Origen emphatically rejects the Docetic doctrine that
Christ's body was not real but an optical illusion, nevertheless he found matter very congenial to his conception
of the varying levels of apprehension of Christ in the
strange doctrine of the apocryphal Acts of John that the
physical appearance of Jesus differed in accordance with
the spiritual insight of the beholder.[24]

The doctrine of differing degrees of knowledge may
be best illustrated by Origen's treatment of the primitive eschatology. The hope of the second coming of
Christ is taken in a literal and material sense by simple
believers. Origen does not attack their belief; it is better
that they should believe the right thing in the wrong
way than not believe it at all, and it is the best of which
they are capable. But the Christian preacher has a
responsibility to educated minds who, so Origen observes, are often distressed by this article of the creed.
The spiritual, symbolic meaning of the doctrine of the
second coming may be either the universal expansion
of the Church throughout the world, bringing all men
to the obedience of Christ, or the inward coming of
Christ to the soul, when he comes not in humiliation
but in glory, uniting the believer to himself in a union
so intense that the believer leaves behind the limitations

of this mortal state and is raised to be one spirit with the Lord.[25] Similarly, Biblical language about punishment for sinners by everlasting fire is understood literally by very simple believers. They do not perceive that the 'fire' of God's judgement is a purifying process which has a remedial end in view; and this is a truth that ought in general to be concealed from them since many can only be deterred from a sinful life by fear. All such Biblical language is an accommodation to them. In truth the fire of judgement has no measurable temperature. Hell is an inner disintegration of the soul, 'a lack of cohesion'.[26] In the *contra Celsum* Origen meets the accusation of Celsus that Christian evangelists stampede people into the Church by frightening them with bogy-words about God as a torturer. He concedes that simple Christians may understand scriptural language about hell in a superstitious and unworthy way. But their error is only to misunderstand the purpose of God. As to the fact they are right: 'we teach about God both what is true and what the multitude can understand, though intelligent Christians understand it in a different sense'. In one sense threats of hell are 'more false than true'. But Plato himself thinks it justifiable to tell a lie to a homicidal lunatic.[27]

Again, the resurrection of the flesh is an article of the creed that some unreflecting Christians understand to mean the resuscitation of this physical body, with all its organs.[28] This belief goes with the literal expectation of the reign of Christ for a thousand years at a renewed Jerusalem.[29] Origen regarded as credible neither the millenarian hope of Christ's return to this earth nor the expectation of a literal resuscitation of this body. He discussed the problem in an early work 'On the Resurrection', of which only sparse fragments have been preserved, so that it is difficult to describe Origen's doctrine without being forced to rely on the onslaughts of his critics, especially Methodius and Jerome, who were certainly less than fair to him. Origen entirely agreed with the numerous pagan critics of the Christian hope as literally interpreted, for example, by Justin or Irenaeus, that no appeal might be made to divine omnipotence to justify affirmations unworthy of God. When St. Paul speaks of powers in heaven as 'bowing the knee' to the Father, we are not to suppose that angels have knees.[30] The risen glory of the redeemed transcends this life. The 'body' will be of a kind appropriate to a heavenly environment.

Perhaps Origen's most important statement about the nature of Christian doctrine as he understands it is contained in his preface to his work 'On First Principles'. He begins by laying down those points of doctrine which are plain and unmistakable because they are given in the rule of faith handed down faithfully in the Church from the apostles. The apostles taught certain doctrines as *credenda*, to be believed without discussion, for they had to provide authoritative affirmations intelligible even to the simplest and most uneducated people. But they often did not state the rational grounds underlying their authoritative affirmations; and there are several questions of some importance for theology on which they gave no clear opinion or guidance. So that there is room for investigation and inquiry on two counts. Authority is not arbitrary, and its justification is the ability to give reasons if required and if the recipient possesses the capacity to comprehend them. On the other hand, where authority has prescribed no particular view, the theologian is free to discuss the issues open to him without having to conform to a fixed rule of thought. The doctrines laid down by the rule of faith as given are the following: (*a*) There is one God who created the world out of nothing, the God of both Old and New Testaments, himself both just and good. (*b*) Jesus Christ is God's pre-existent Son, begotten before all worlds, who, without ceasing to be God, became man, born of a virgin and the Holy Spirit; he truly suffered and died, rose again, and ascended to heaven. (*c*) The Holy Spirit is of like rank, but it is not clearly stated in scripture whether he is uncreated or whether he belongs to the created order. What is certain is that the Holy Spirit inspired the Biblical writers. (*d*) The soul will be rewarded for its actions with heaven or hell, and there will be a resurrection of the dead. It is certain that free will must be affirmed. But nothing in scripture makes it clear how the soul comes to be united to the body—whether it is transmitted from the parents together with the seed that grows into the body, or whether it comes into the body from outside, or whether it is created by God or uncreated and immortal. (*e*) It is certain that the devil and evil angels exist. How they came to be and who they are is obscure, though most

Christians (of whom Origen is one) think the devil an apostate angel. (*f*) It is certain that this material world was made at a definite time, and will suffer dissolution one day. But it is not clear what existed before it or what will be after it. (*g*) It is certain that scripture is inspired by God and has a meaning deeper than the literal sense; but the elucidation of the true inner meaning is a problem left to the expositor. (*h*) It is not clear beyond discussion whether God and indeed all souls are immaterial beings or whether they have some shape like that of physical bodies. And cognate questions are raised by Church teaching about guardian angels and by the question whether the sun, moon, and stars are ensouled (as the Platonists say) or not.

The presuppositions of this preliminary statement are evidently very different from those governing Irenaeus's theology. For Irenaeus heresy comes of following the itch to speculate where scripture has given no clear guidance; we must be content not to know if the word of God is not explicit, and should maintain as reverent an agnosticism in matters of high theology as we are bound to hold about the causes of bird migration or the sources of the Nile or other matters of natural philosophy which lie beyond the reach of human inquiry.[31] Reason is confronted by a definite frontier, and is precluded from crossing that frontier by the limitations of human knowledge unless it is given in the Bible manifest authority to think about those questions that transcend creaturely capacities. It is the error of the Gnostics that they claim to know what we are not meant to know. Origen is as conscious as Irenaeus of the limitations of human intellectual powers for inquiring into the transcendental world, but thinks it possible for the human mind, with the aid of grace given in answer to prayer and purity of heart, to speculate with becoming diffidence even about questions that are not explicitly set out in the apostolic rule of faith.

Origen begins by eliminating the anthropomorphic notion that God is literally light or fire or spirit in a Stoic sense of a tenuous thinking gas. God is the immaterial ground of being, the cause of all that is. To be is to participate in him who is. He is alone underived, the Monad, transcending all multiplicity, self-sufficient, and beyond the power of the human mind unaided by special grace. In one passage[32] Celsus commends to the Christians a study of Plato if they want to find a reliable theologian: the Platonic school distinguishes three ways in which the knowledge of God is attainable by man, namely, the *via eminentiae* affirming that the highest we know is the least that may be predicated of God, the *via negativa* defining him in terms of what he is not, and the way of analogy, as when we say that God is to the intelligible world what the sun is to the visible and sensible world, making it possible for the eye to see the phenomenal world and indeed itself as well. Origen replies that more than rational dialectic is required for the knowledge of God: 'Human nature is not sufficient to find God unless it is helped by God who is the object of the search; and he is found by those who, after doing all that they can, admit that they need him. He shows himself to those to whom he judges it right to appear, so far as it is possible for God to be known to man and for the human soul which is still in the body to know God.' God is known by a free act of grace on his part, and he reveals himself to those who are pure in heart (so that holiness is an essential requirement, not merely dialectics) through the incarnate Logos. With this large qualification Origen would happily approve of Celsus's statement. The discussion with Celsus illustrates well the double-sided character of Origen's doctrine of God. On the one side he takes for granted the transcendentalist theology of Platonism, that God is the ground of being and even 'beyond being', in need of nothing, though the cosmos has come into being by an overflow of the divine nature which is goodness. On the other side Origen is trying to make room within this scheme for the idea of freedom in God and also in the creatures, and for the notion of a gulf between the infinite Creator and the finite creatures which, by virtue of being created, are strictly dependent and transitory except in so far as they are kept in being by the will of their Maker.

Creation is the consequence of an overflow of divine goodness, its initial object being the order of rational beings, pure spirits unencumbered with material bodies like ours. Since there can never have been a time when divine goodness and power were inactive, there is a sense in which this spiritual cosmos is eternal. If it is not eternally necessary to the being of God, it is certainly an eternal consequence of his nature. Nevertheless

Origen also asserts that these rational, spiritual beings are creatures, not uncreated but dependent on the divine will for their existence. Origen is well aware that he is confronting an insoluble problem in trying to reconcile the affirmation that creation is an outflow of the divine nature with the affirmation that it is dependent on a free decision of the divine will. But the affirmation that the discarnate rational beings eternally exist as a correlate of the eternity of the Creator's goodness seems to Origen to be a necessary assertion if the immutability of God is to be upheld. It is on this same ground that he affirms that the generation of the Son is not a temporal act or a moment in a succession of events, but an eternal generation. The Father is eternally Father; there was never a time when the Son was not. Unless this assertion is made, the unchangeableness of God is prejudiced.

The Logos is the image of the Father's power—not an image of the Father so identical with the archetype that he can be said to be as much Father as the Father himself.[33] All rational beings participate in the rationality of the divine Reason who is the archetypal source of their nature, and the mediator between the Father and the creatures. The Logos is therefore God in relation to the lower order; he is God immanent.

The rational beings so created were not self-sufficient, but were turned towards God in adoration. But they came to neglect their love for God. Following an idea suggested by Philo[34] Origen says that they became 'sated' and so fell. By falling from the divine love they cooled and so perhaps became 'souls'[35]—for *psyche* was commonly derived from *psychesthai* by an etymology as old as Plato and Aristotle and exploited by the Stoics who thought that as a newborn baby emerged to the cold air it gasped for its first breath and that at this point the soul first entered its body. To Origen the Pauline trichotomy of body, soul, and spirit suggested that the soul was midway between matter and spirit; it might descend to materialism, but it was called to unite with the highest element, the *pneuma*, and thereby to cease to be *psyche*.[36] (To Origen's later critics this entire notion of spirits falling to become souls seemed very damaging, but the point is not really of central importance for Origen's own thought.)

Origen's next speculation is an adventurous step. He proposes to regard the diversity of spiritual entities, stretching downwards from the archangels through inferior angelic powers and saints to men and yet lower still to demonic powers, as constituting a hierarchy of consubstantial rational beings, which is brought about not, as many of the contemporary Platonists said, by an evolutionary process of necessary emanations from above but by free will being exercised in different ways.[37] The material world is created by God through the Logos by whose power the immense diversity of the hierarchy of being is controlled and so prevented from disintegration. The sensible world is created by God out of nothing, by which Origen means absolute, not merely relative, non-being. 'I cannot understand how so many eminent men have imagined matter to be uncreated.'[38]

Origen is strongly critical of the Platonic doctrine of the eternity of the visible world. The words of *Timaeus* 41 that, although the cosmos is created and so in principle destructible, yet in practice by God's will it will never be destroyed, hold good according to Origen not of this phenomenal world but only of that higher world of discarnate spiritual beings, the realm of saints and angels. Origen likewise rejects the teaching of the *Timaeus* that while the transcendent God is the source and maker of gods derived from himself it is these inferior powers who are responsible for the material world.[39] This doctrine of the *Timaeus* had been freely accepted by Philo, and used by him as an explanation of the problem of evil.[40] But for Origen this view was hopelessly gnostic in its implications, and he would have none of it. In arguing against Celsus he decisively rejects the view that evil inheres in matter, and underlines the point when he says that the Christian doctrine of God as creating matter does not in any way make him responsible for evil.[41]

Nevertheless, Origen never reaches a perfectly clear and decisive opinion on the exact status of matter in the divine purpose, even though the solution of this problem is of the highest importance both for his conception of the nature of man and for his doctrine of the destiny of the redeemed. He reviews three possibilities, but the discussion does not arrive at a decision.[42] First, there is the view that matter is eternal and that it will suffer an eschatological transformation, in which case the resurrection body will be in form like our earthly body but

glorified and radiant. Secondly, it is possible that discarnate spirits can exist without any bodies of any kind
whatever, though they may need bodies for a time at a
certain stage of their education on the way back to God.
If so, the material order will be brought into existence
as required, which may be from time to time since progress upward may not be constant and there may be
occasional set-backs and manifestations of recalcitrance
to the divine will. Thirdly, there is the possibility that
the visible and corruptible part of the world will be
entirely destroyed, but the glorious spirits in the upper
spheres of the cosmos may come to have yet more
glorious forms than they already possess. Origen
simply submits these three views to the reader's judgement. His own sympathy lies more perhaps with either
the second or third than the first.[43] There are places in
his commentaries where he implies the third view with
its implication that all created spirits are in some degree
involved in corporeality; in the case of angels (he remarks) the matter of their body will not be heavy and
weighed down like ours on this earth, but will be
ethereal, like the astral body of which the Neoplatonists
speculated; and in principle, it is implied, only the
Trinity is intrinsically incorporeal, so that if we speak
of angels as 'incorporeal' we mean that they are relatively incorporeal in comparison with us.[44]

This way of thinking of the nature of matter is of
course quite remote from our modern notions. But
Origen is only giving expression to ideas which were
widely assumed by a large number of his Platonizing

contemporaries. The whole conception was made easier for him by the current dogma that in itself matter is without form or qualities, a common substratum, upon which various qualities may be imposed in accordance with the archetypal ideas. So the universal, which is the form or species, is imposed on qualityless matter to make each individual thing or animal what it is. To Platonists who objected to the doctrine of the resurrection of the body Origen had an unanswerable argument based precisely on his opponents' presuppositions: why should not the Creator impose a fresh form on the same common matter, so preserving continuity with the personality in this life, while making its new form appropriate to its environment?[45]

Nevertheless, Origen's attitude towards matter is much less positive than Clement's. He is inclined to think that the sun, moon, and stars are ensouled by spiritual beings who, having fallen a certain distance from God, have been incarcerated in these physical bodies, to us very splendid, but a degradation so far as they are concerned, and commanded to indicate to human beings on earth the passing of time.[46] Origen will not accept the gnostic use of astrology, but St. Paul's words about the creation being subjected to futility in hope of deliverance from the bondage of corruption seemed to him to reinforce his view that all spiritual beings, now imprisoned in material bodies, yearn to ascend higher and pray for a release which they cannot be granted before the proper time. Like the apostle in prison they long to depart, but realize that to abide in the flesh is more needful to assist inferior beings.

Certainly this material world is beautiful and noble and shows evidence of its design by a beneficent Creator. But it is not comfortable and is not intended to be. Man is put here as in 'a place of affliction' to educate him to return to his Maker.[47] It would not be good for him to live in a world from which all accidents and all pain are excluded. Natural catastrophes like earthquakes, famines, and plagues may shorten life, but such disasters do not count against the goodness of God, however purposeless they may seem at the time to the sufferers. Many virtues come out of adversity.[48] Evil inheres not in the natural order, but in the resistant will of the creatures.

Clement had regarded sex and marriage as a major crux in the conflict between the Church and Gnosticism, and had emphatically asserted the goodness of the natural order as the gift of God. Origen's tone is markedly different. It is true that he rejects the strict Encratite notion that marriage is incompatible with the profession of the Christian faith, and tolerates second marriages for weaker brethren. But his ascetic mind does not think kindly of the married state. Marriage is inferior to celibacy—on the two grounds, long familiar in pagan thought and by implication (even if it is not stated in so many words) almost given canonical authority within Christianity by St. Paul in 1 Corinthians vii, that sexual intercourse is a defilement interfering with the elevation of the soul above this material

world to the realm of spirit, and that one who has dedicated himself to the love of God must forgo the love of
mortals. Origen protests that the sexual impulse is
indeed natural and instinctive, not (as some Christians
think) of diabolical prompting; but it is instinctive in
the sense that anger is: sin is inextricably bound up with
it.[49] So the priest who offers the Church's sacrifice must
be pure.[50] In Origen's time there is no general demand
for clerical celibacy as yet, and his demand is addressed
to married clergy as much as to unmarried. Conjugal
relations in marriage are for the purpose of procreation,
and otherwise are disallowed as mere self-indulgence.[51]
Because there is a defilement attaching to the reproduc-
tive process, the Church baptizes infants.[52] When in
Romans v. 14 St. Paul speaks of 'sin in the likeness of
Adam's transgression', the simple exegesis is that the
universal sinfulness of society is due not to heredity but
to environment and education. But deeper inquirers
will understand the text to mean that somehow all men
existed in Adam's loins and suffered expulsion from
paradise with him.[53] All are born impure. In the Bible
the only two who celebrate their birthday are Pharaoh
and Herod.[54] The purity and sinlessness of Jesus, however, was ensured by the Virgin Birth.[55] Perhaps under
the influence of Clement's denial of the notion, Origen
reaches no decision about the Philonic and gnostic
interpretation of the 'coats of skins' with which Adam
and Eve were clothed after their fall: they may be
bodies, but this is not certain.[56] But the entire tendency
of Origen's ethic is to build on the antithesis of spirit and

matter and to think of the way of moral and spiritual advance as a progressive suppression of the mind's responsiveness to the pull of the flesh. Just as in the soul's advance in the spiritual life it comes to understand the mysteries of theology in a deeper way than it did at earlier stages, so also it comes to have a deeper grasp of the nature of sin, so that actions which at the beginning were not regarded as sinful come to be seen in their true light.[57]

The model for the Christian's spiritual progress is not merely the strenuous self-discipline of the prophets but supremely the incarnate Lord. Among all the rational beings originally made by God there was one which inflexibly adhered to the divine love without wavering.[58] This soul was taken to be united to the Logos in a union as inseparable as that of iron in a white-hot fire. (The illustration, it should be said, is a commonplace analogy of Stoic philosophy to describe the union of soul and body as one of complete interpenetration). Even the body which the Logos took of Mary was caught up into the union so that the divine and human united to become one Christ.[59] By this union the properties of the humanity of Christ may be ascribed to the divine Logos and vice versa.[60] The full humanity of Christ is essential for our salvation, and any part of our threefold nature of body, soul, and spirit not assumed by the Logos is not saved.[61] He possessed a soul of the same substance as all other souls,[62] and is our example as man,[63] but this does not mean that he is a mere man or that he is elevated to divine rank by adoption.[64] He is the pre-existent eternal Logos through whom we pray to the Father,[65] one whom we may even, with appropriate qualifications and explanations, describe as a 'second God' beside the Father.[66] For the Father and the Son are one in power and in will, but differ in their *hypostasis*[67]—and even, as Origen also says, in their *ousia*, though the context makes it clear that this word is being used as virtually synonymous with *hypostasis* on this occasion.[68] Origen is vehemently opposed to the modalist Monarchianism which regarded Father, Son, and Spirit as adjectival names to describe the one divine substance and formally denied that God is in himself three.

The incarnate Lord is the pattern and model for the salvation of humanity. 'With Jesus human and divine nature began to be woven together, so that by sharing with divine life human nature might become divine, not only in Jesus but also in all believers.'[69] So salvation is deification. This means the annihilation not of individuality but of the gulf between finite and infinite. Nor does it mean that the believer, following Christ as example, can find his mystical way to God independently of Christ. 'Even at the very highest climax of contemplation we do not for a moment forget the incarnation.'[70] While the Incarnation is a veritable revelation of God, it is the ladder by which we are to ascend from the flesh to the spirit, from the Son of Man to the Son of God. The incarnate Lord, like the written revelation in inspired scripture, is a veil that must be penetrated.[71] It is an accommodation to our present capacities in this life. The Church's present gospel will one day be superseded by that which the Seer of the Apocalypse calls the everlasting gospel, a heavenly comprehension of truth that will surpass our present understanding by at least as much as the new covenant surpasses the old.[72] But throughout the period of this mortal life we are dependent on the sacramental, external forms of Bible and Church; secondary as they may be, they are an indispensable vehicle.[73]

The Church is a school, making many concessions to weaker brethren, but always seeking to elevate them to higher things and a more intelligent degree of theological literacy. The Christian preacher's task is to rebuke and to encourage, above all to move to penitence.[74] Advance comes as we confess our sins to spiritual advisers, who in Origen's view are to be clergy; but spiritual power is not always conjoined with ecclesiastical authority, though it ought to be, and the power of the keys is only truly possessed by them if their formal authority is coupled with personal holiness.[75]

This process of education is not confined to this life. None is so pure that at death he is fit for the presence of God.[76] Therefore there will be purification hereafter, in which God will purge away the wood, hay, and stubble erected on the foundation laid by Christ.[77] The atonement is a long-continuing process[78] in which Christ is conquering the powers of evil assaulting the soul. Moreover, the very powers of evil themselves are not outside the reach of his care. The beings who are now devils were not created so. They were created good by nature, like all other spiritual beings, and have become evil only in will.[79] It is a gnostic doctrine that any creature of God can become so totally depraved as to become incapable of any goodness at all. 'A totally depraved being could not be censured, but only pitied as a poor unfortunate.'[80] Even the prince of darkness himself retains some vestige of a capacity to recognize truth, some remnants of freedom and some rationality. No creature of God ever passes wholly beyond the bounds of his love and judgement. Origen is emphatic that redemption is not a naturalistic process moving onward of its own motion by an inevitable destiny. Rebels from God remain for ever free to refuse. But the atoning work of Christ is incomplete until all are redeemed, and 'love never fails'.[81] The process of redemption may take more than one 'age', but the ultimate triumph will surely be God's.[82] Even so, freedom is inalienable from the rational being; if the spiritual creatures once suffered satiety and fell, there can be in principle no ground for denying the possibility that they may fall again. If so, there may be a series of worlds in which providence has to redeem a fallen creation and bring it back to its Maker.[83] Or may we affirm that at the final restoration love will be indefectible, and that those who have seen the glory of the kingdom will never taste of death?[84]

THE PERENNIAL ISSUE

NURSERY memory recalls a rhyme about a little girl who had a little curl right in the middle of her forehead. It proceeds to give an estimate of her moral variability which bears a striking resemblance to the judgement on Origen which we find in the traditions of both Eastern and Western Christendom. In a fifteenth-century Greek manuscript in the Vatican library there is a marginal note written by George Scholarius, the Byzantine philosopher and theologian who under the name of Gennadius II became the first patriarch of Constantinople under the Turks:

The Western writers say, 'Where Origen was good, no one is better, where he was bad, no one is worse.' Our Asian divines say on the one hand that 'Origen is the whetstone of us all', but on the other hand, that 'he is the fount of foul doctrines'.

Scholarius continues with the comment:

Both are right: he splendidly defended Christianity, wonderfully expounded scripture, and wrote a noble exhortation to martyrdom. But he was also the father of Arianism, and worst of all, said that hellfire would not last for ever.[1]

The name of Origen never fails to be divisive. It is curious to notice how throughout the long history of

Christian thought Origen and his teaching are continually coming to the surface in one form or another. Dismissed as a heretic by a Jerome or a Justinian, he will be sure to return in Didymus and Evagrius or in the Palestinian monks of Justinian's time[2] or in the mystical speculations of an Eriugena, a Nicolas of Cusa, or even a Berdyaev. Ever since the main theses of 'Origenism' (as we must call it, without forgetting that it is a genuine question whether, or rather in what sense, Origen himself is an Origenist) were condemned under Justinian at the fifth General Council,[3] it has been disputed whether Origen could be saved. Dangerous views concerning the salvability of Origen involved Pico della Mirandola in acute embarrassments in a famous controversy of Renaissance times.[4] In the present century there have been several manifestations of sympathy for Origen especially in France on the Catholic side, as in the writings of Fr. Henri de Lubac, Fr. Crouzel, and Fr. Daniélou. In England during the discussions of the twenties concerning the revision of the Book of Common Prayer the Anglo-Catholic, Dr. Darwell Stone, urged that the name of Origen should be inserted in the Anglican Calendar as a saint.[5] But the old misgivings have continued to be voiced, and no sooner is the case stated for the defence than there appears a fresh attack from the prosecution. No discussion of Origen can proceed far without coming back to the perennial problem of his orthodoxy. All other questions appear ultimately secondary to this. And the problem did not first come into existence only as a result of the sharper definition of orthodoxy after the controversies of the fourth and fifth centuries. The protagonists of orthodoxy against Arian and Apollinarian heresy were well aware that Christian writers of the second and third centuries had often failed to express themselves with that precision which heretical depravity was now making necessary. They were troubled not by occasional indiscretions or innocent lapses but by the whole temper and structure of Origen's speculations.

Even during his lifetime his teaching was a stone of stumbling to some, while to others it seemed that he and he alone could fully expound the glories of the Christian tradition in a way that conceded nothing to gnostic heresy and yet went beyond the simple, mythological, and eschatological language of the catechism and the baptismal creed. 'There are some', he once complains, 'who love me beyond measure and laud my teaching to the skies. Others slander my writings and accuse me of doctrines which I do not hold.'[6] Origen approves of his uncritical admirers as little as of his hostile slanderers. Like Augustine, he is continually asking his hearers and readers to be critical and to subject his work to correction if they find it inadequate. When Jerome in his early days of ecstatic enthusiasm for Origen described him as 'the greatest teacher of the Church since the apostles',[7] he was echoing language such as earlier admirers had used.[8] And the opposition complained that Origen's friends seemed to think his works on a par with those of the prophets and apostles.[9] Origen was aware of his critics. He refers to those who laughed at his allegories as mere subjectivism and fancy,[10] and who insisted that historical matter must be treated as historical.[11] Once he sympathizes with Jeremiah when the prophet decided to keep silence in face of the surrounding critics ready to pick on his words, and observes that it is a temptation he has often felt himself: 'If it gets me into trouble when I teach and preach, why do I not rather retire to the desert and to quiet?'[12] His critics were of course entirely right in seeing allegory as an indispensable tool without which Origen could not find what he wanted in scripture. The modern reader, conditioned to regard all allegory as nothing but a dishonest sophistication designed to evade difficulties in a sacred text, is often not as sympathetic as an historical point of view would demand towards a man who can find his ideas almost anywhere in the most improbable passages. It is hard for us to appreciate the degree to which allegory made it possible both for an ancient text to be made contemporary and for human thought to be free to develop without being constricted by a rigid authority. Like Philo, Origen simply and sincerely believed that the Bible was intended by its divine author to be expounded in more than one sense, and he endeavoured to formulate some objective rules for interpretation.[13] Not all the rules that he framed are likely to impress a modern reader, but the fact that he made the attempt is significant.

But the main contemporary gravamen against him was not on account of his expository method but on account of his doctrine, in particular his eschatology. About the

year 229 Origen, who was continually being invited to
visit other churches to give lectures, and in some cases
even to preach until Bishop Demetrius of Alexandria
protested against putting a layman into the pulpit, was
asked to go to Greece to help the church at Athens in
refuting a troublesome Valentinian heretic named Candidus. It was while he was on his journey thither that
he passed through Caesarea in Palestine and there
accepted ordination to the presbyterate at the hands of
the local bishop.[14] At Athens the dispute with Candidus
turned on the nature and destiny of the devil. The
Valentinian argued that the orthodox admitted the
fundamental principle of Gnosticism in the dualism
implied by their view of the devil as one to be eternally
damned and as beyond the very possibility of redemption. Origen replied to this with his usual argument that
the devil fell by will; to say that he is evil by nature and
constitution is to find fault with the Creator, and true
Christianity rejects any ultimate dualism; therefore it is
possible for even the devil to be saved.[15] The publication
by Candidus of his version of the disputation came as
a bombshell.[16] At Alexandria Bishop Demetrius, in-
censed by the act of his brother bishop of Caesarea in
laying hands on Origen without so much as consulting
him, saw in Origen's doctrine unambiguous evidence
of grave heresy and proceeded to denounce him. Origen
cannot have poured oil on the stormy waters when he
wrote to his friends at Alexandria that, just as Michael
the archangel did not bring a railing accusation against
the devil, so he thought it wrong to speak evil of the

devil—any more, indeed, than of Demetrius and those who had condemned him.[17] When he returned to Alexandria he found that all work was impossible. The shorthand writers normally provided for him at the expense of his friend Ambrose refused to work for him, and in 231 he decided to migrate to Caesarea in the spirit of the children of Israel migrating from the bondage of Pharaoh.[18] The Palestinian bishops were glad to give asylum to a distinguished theologian and eloquent preacher who, as they saw it, had been so hopelessly misunderstood by his uninstructed ecclesiastical superior. Their action raised large issues of custom and church order with regard to the reception to communion in one church of one who had been expelled from another, and an irate correspondence ensued, in which Origen wrote to Bishop Fabian of Rome to defend himself.[19] He evidently thought that Demetrius had acted hastily without even understanding the point at issue, a charge in which there was probably much truth.[20] The fourth-century defenders of Origen, however, significantly keep silence on the doctrinal point, and explain Demetrius's hostility as motivated by personal envy and his canonical censure as based on strictly technical objections to the Palestinian ordination.

Writing in 374–5 Epiphanius concludes his immense attack on Origen's heresy with the summary charge that Origen was 'blinded by Greek culture' (*paideia*).[21] The accusation raises large questions: was Origen's deviation from the path of orthodoxy caused by his incorporation of pagan ideas within ecclesiastical doctrine? Did he produce a hellenized version of Christianity that was seriously influential in converting the educated classes of society in the eastern provinces of the Empire?

Epiphanius's charge needs to be tested against Origen's attitude to Greek philosophy as expressed in his own writings. For of the early Christian theologians whose work we have briefly surveyed in these lectures Origen is outstanding not for the friendliness of his utterances about Greek philosophy but for the opposite.

In Justin we saw Greek philosophy and Christianity set in an amicable juxtaposition without any hard words or accusations on the Christian side and with the quiet, courteous assumption that Christianity is the fulfilment towards which philosophy, like the Old Testament itself, was always pointing, even if it did not know it. In Clement this relationship has become rather less simple, and so far as outward appearance goes less benevolent, even if Clement expresses his reserve with urbanity and a proper respect for the conventions of contemporary rhetoric. Yet at the same time as the outward friendliness is cooler, the intellectual reconciliation has inwardly become much deeper and more intimate. Clement's doctrine of God is more deeply impregnated with Platonic transcendentalism than Justin's; and whereas Justin's theology is popular Christianity with a strong eschatology of the most unsymbolic kind, Clement has an eschatology which has been drastically transmuted either into a Johannine existentialism or into symbolist utterance about the destiny of the soul at the climax of its ascent to union with God. It is characteristic that the gospel saying 'Watch, for you know not in what hour the Son of Man comes' has become for Clement a warning about the enervating effects of lying too long in bed.[22]

In comparison with Clement, Origen's overt attitude towards classical Greek philosophy is even more reserved and critical; nevertheless, there is in one sense an even profounder synthesis between Christianity and Platonism. This is in part related to a temperamental difference between the two men. Clement is a cultivated man of letters using philosophy for his own purposes, directing his writings not at an audience of professional philosophers but at well-educated and intelligent people whose culture is more literary than philosophical. A poet is at least as likely as a philosopher to have expressed the religious truth that Clement is seeking for—though probably Clement would not have gone so far as to echo Horace's dictum that one learns much more about morality from Homer than from philosophers.[23]

Origen does not belong to the polite literary world of dinner-party conversation which is mirrored in Clement's pages. He has no desire to do so. A stern ascetic with an insatiable appetite for incessant work which earned him the nickname Adamantius,[24] he would not have been an entirely comfortable and relaxed person with whom to spend a pleasant conversational evening. He is not indeed without feeling for literature, and can quote his Homer as well as anyone when he wishes.[25] But he does not often so wish. He regards philosophy as incomparably more important than drama or poetry, and in handling the opinions of the different philosophical schools he moves with the easy familiarity of a master. He knows just how to set one school against another, how the subtleties of the Stoics can be met by the ingenuity of the Academics and Peripatetics, or vice versa. But towards even the philosophers his attitude is distant, and he can use expressions of cold disparagement which strike the reader as odd in view of the entirely Greek cast of his mind. His manner struck Porphyry, who was directly and emotionally involved, as offensive and unpardonable, and he could only regard Origen as a crook who used Greek tools to rationalize a crude barbarian superstition, having apostatized from the faith in which he had been brought up. Porphyry's accusation presupposes that no one could be as deeply hellenized as Origen without accepting the polytheistic belief with which, for him, Hellenic culture was indissolubly associated.[26]

Underneath the cold language much of the detail of Origen's use of philosophy is in line with the programme laid down by Justin and developed by Clement. 'Every wise man, to the extent that he is wise, participates in Christ who is wisdom.'[27] The Logos lights every man coming into the world, and all beings that are rational share in the true light. It is the Holy Spirit, not the Logos, whose work is confined to the Church, which explains why some Greek philosophers say the world was created by the Logos of God but have no inkling of the Holy Spirit.[28] Man is made in the image of the Logos,[29] possessing as his eternal birthright freedom and rationality, the capacity to recognize the good, and the desire for God. This yearning for the source of his being is universal in man; and Origen, almost like Coleridge or Schleiermacher, argues that this sense of aching need cannot have been implanted in the heart of man unless it is capable of being satisfied. Each of our five physical senses is related to a specific category of objects; so also the human mind is the correlate of God and is made for God.[30] When the Lord declared that 'the kingdom of heaven is within you' he meant just this: discover the image of God within your own soul by introspection and withdrawing the mind from the distractions of sense.[31] It is coherent with this that Origen freely accepts the Stoic conception of 'universal notions' as a source of truth. It is the general consensus of all rational men that a spiritual religion is incompatible with crude idolatry and polytheistic practice.[32] This instance is noteworthy; Origen appeals to the 'universal notions' to criticize pagan religion, but never invokes them to justify some modification or reinterpretation of the baptismal faith.

Celsus once complains that Christians have nothing new to say in their ethical teaching, and that the classical philosophers said it all long ago.[33] Origen's reply is remarkable. He simply accepts the proposition without demur. So far from Christianity being the worse for that, it is evidence in its favour. Every man has an innate awareness of what is right and wrong. 'Do you not judge for yourselves what is right?'[34] Any open-minded reader of the Sermon on the Mount will agree that its recommendations and counsels accord with an ideal pattern for human relations. The gospel is a republication of the law of nature implanted by creation. It does not bring a new morality, but a recognition of the divine righteousness and love as the underlying ground of the highest ethical aspiration.[35] So the gospel brings to actuality what is present in man potentially, and its 'newness' consists in the concrete example of Christ himself. The Greek philosophers speak of modesty, the Bible of humility.[36] It is the same thing, but humility is found in a relation of love to God. This does not mean that for Origen a natural prudential morality is enough. He (hesitantly) denies the saving value before God of good works done before justification,[37] and in no degree mitigates the absoluteness of the Christian faith as revelation. There is salvation only in Christ, and all must come, sooner or later, to this realization, in the next world if not in this.[38] So Origen combines an estimate of human nature which is strikingly positive and 'humanist' with a cool reserve towards the good pagan.[39] He can refer with some sympathy to the familiar Stoic paradoxes that the wise man alone is free and noble and kingly; but the reference is not enthusiastic, for he goes on to add, coolly enough, that perhaps at some other time he will 'consider' the degree to which a Christian can accept them.[40]

Towards the materialism of Stoic metaphysics Origen is as hostile as any Platonist, and he censures, like Justin and Clement, the Stoics' pantheism and deterministic doctrine of world-cycles.[41] In the *contra Celsum* he once draws a sharp distinction between the cosmic vitalism of the Stoics and the Christian conception of God's immanent providence as a power directed by a transcendent will.[42] The point of closest contact between Origen and Stoicism appears in his free use of the arsenal of argument forged by Chrysippus in defence of providence and especially in justification of the doctrine that the rational beings in the cosmos are the object of special care. Like Justin and Clement before him, Origen stresses without apology the anthropocentric purpose of the created world. To all three men the proposition seemed essential to any adequate understanding of the Incarnation and the divine purpose for the salvation of man. It is no accident that some of Celsus's most elaborate argument is directed at just this point. For the pagan Platonist the refutation of the Christian thesis requires an extended argument to prove that animals are not less rational than human beings. The argument was a well-worn theme in the debates between Academic and Stoic philosophers of the hellenistic age. Like Philo, who devoted an entire tract to the question, Origen decisively identifies himself with the Stoic side of the argument. The modern reader of this discussion of animal rationality in the fourth book of the *contra Celsum* is likely to be overwhelmed by a sense of the extraordinary futility of the arguments used by both participants. Yet underlying the apparently trivial and often absurd arguments about the religious beliefs of elephants or the filial devotion of storks there is more to be considered than the way in which this kind of nonsense was continued in the *Physiologus* and the compilers of medieval bestiaries. The latent question at issue is that of the transcendence of man in relation to his environment and to his own animal nature. When Celsus levels man down to the irrational creatures, Origen replies that his argument is derogatory to the dignity of man created in the image of God and is in principle destructive in its moral consequences.[43]

Origen's intimate knowledge of Stoic logic and ethics is evident throughout his writings, and he had certainly read for himself many of the works of Chrysippus and some of the recorded discourses of Musonius Rufus and Epictetus. Of some points in Stoic doctrine it is no exaggeration to say that they are first made fully intelligible to the historian of philosophy by Origen's expositions and comments. But although there is much knowledge of Stoicism and an evident debt to the Stoic theodicy, it is a mistake to overestimate this Stoic element in his mental furniture and to label him an adherent. Origen, like Clement before him, illustrates the general tendency of eclectic Platonism in his time, incorporating Stoic ethics within a Platonist metaphysic. Moreover, like Philo he found himself ranged with the Stoics against the Sceptics on the question of providence and in affirming that the cosmos is so ordered as to favour right moral action.[44] When he had himself suffered expulsion from his Alexandrian home on grounds that he thought wholly unreasonable, he made his own the old Stoic language that happiness is inward and independent of external circumstances.[45] But Origen's divergence from the Stoics appears not only in his doctrine of God but also in his anthropology. For while he was happy to accept the Stoic recipe for happiness, that one should limit desire to that which no external power can remove or disturb, yet he did not think that the soul possessed in itself any inherent quality of moral immutability, and was far more deeply aware of its frailty and weakness. For Origen the mutability of the soul is only overcome as it is united to God by grace.[46] If there is an obvious surface similarity between the Stoic doctrine of world-cycles and Origen's speculative notions, it must also be recognized that the Stoic doctrine rested on a deterministic conception, while it was a thoroughgoing libertarianism which compelled Origen to allow for at least the hypothetical possibility that the redeemed might not for ever exercise their will rightly, so that even where he seemed to agree with the Stoics it was for diametrically opposed reasons.[47]

In the Cappadocian Fathers of the fourth century it is a conventional accusation against the Arians that they apply the profane logic of Aristotle to the ineffable mystery of the holy Trinity.[48] It would be difficult to discern any deep or direct influence of Aristotelian thought on Origen's mind.[49] In this respect Origen's position is similar to that of the second-century Platonist Atticus, large quotations from whom are preserved by Eusebius of Caesarea. Atticus was writing to refute those fellow-Platonists who believed they had found a way to reconcile Plato with Aristotle.[50] His objections to Aristotle closely coincide with those of Origen: Aristotle fails to see that happiness must be found solely in virtue, not in physical well-being or external circumstances; he denies the effective care of providence for human affairs, and so denies both the value of prayer and man's answerability hereafter for his actions; he denies that the world is created; he denies the immortality of the soul and holds that the ether is of a fifth, unchangeable essence, beside the four elements of earth, water, air, and fire. Excellent as a guide to terrestrial facts, he is a weak and blind guide on transcendental realities.[51] These complaints by Atticus recur in Origen. Origen was aware of Christian theologians who sought to expound the harmony of Aristotle with the Bible. The task was probably not more difficult than harmonizing him with Plato, as those opposed by Atticus wished to do, and as Ammonius Saccas is specifically reported to have done.[52] At any rate, in his commentary on Psalm iv Origen makes an attack on Christian exegetes who find in Scripture support for the 'Aristotelian' opinion that goodness is not only moral but is also a matter of the body and of external things.[53] It was conventionally claimed for Aristotle's philosophy that it adopted a 'more human' standpoint than its rivals. Origen did not deem this to be a merit.[54] Nor is he seriously interested in Aristotelian logic, though well acquainted with the usual logical conundrums of the schools. He once gives a verbatim quotation from the *Categories*,[55] and occasionally quotes an Aristotelian definition,[56] though these are more likely to be derived from school handbooks summarizing philosophical opinions than from the original writings of Aristotle himself. Origen's identification of the Christian attitude to Aristotle with that adopted by a strict Platonist like Atticus is not surprising. The Aristotelian conception that birth and wealth may be held to contribute to the good life as well as moral virtue was not likely to be congenial to a Christian of the age of the martyrs. The notion that providence becomes progressively less effective as it descends towards terrestrial affairs could not be reconciled with a divine revelation culminating in incarnation. On one point, perhaps, Origen might have been expected to have sympathy for Aristotle, namely, in his doctrine that the ether of the heavens is composed of a fifth essence, not of the four elements of which this lower world is constituted. For this could have appealed to a theologian reputed to hold that the resurrection body is wholly discontinuous with the physical frame to which the soul is linked in this life. The Aristotelian doctrine of the fifth essence was resolutely opposed by Stoic exponents of cosmic 'sympathy',[57] as also by Atticus and the orthodox Platonists. It is important for Origen's doctrine of the resurrection to notice that he is consistently determined to reject the Aristotelian doctrine precisely on the ground that the Christian belief in the resurrection excludes it, and that it implies a depreciation of the status of the physical body. Some Peripatetic philosophers held that the soul is of the ethereal fifth essence.[58] It is material evidence that Origen is not quite as 'spiritualizing' in his doctrine of the resurrection as some later critics imagined that he never considers this doctrine as a possible view, and never tries to interpret the faith in the life of the world to come by drawing on Aristotelian conceptions of the soul as being derived from the stuff of the heavens.[59]

The extent of Origen's indebtedness to Plato is a complex and delicate matter. In substantial respects Platonism is in the air that he and his contemporaries breathe, and it is therefore beyond criticism. He takes for granted the Platonist's conception of the metaphysical structure of the world, and assumes without discussion that the cosmos is divided into higher and lower, eternal and temporal, intelligible and sensible, spirit and matter. The world of sense is to become the means by which, and from which, we must rise to apprehend the world of truth and ultimate value, where wisdom and knowledge are the only sure and abiding realities.[60] Origen sees this principle exemplified in the Incarnation, in the place of the sacraments in the life of the Church, and in the Bible where the inward spirit is veiled in, with, and under the external letter of law, history, and parable. Inevitably he finds himself in an ambivalent position regarding the external and the historical. In the fourth book 'On First Principles' he first argues at length that the true meaning of scripture must be the spiritual and allegorical meaning, since there are statements in the Bible which are literally and historically impossible.

The argument is then qualified by the remark that this does not mean that none of the Bible is history, that no laws are to be understood literally, or that no records of events in the life of Christ are to be taken as history.[61] It is only relatively few passages that have no literal meaning at all, and they are providentially placed in scripture to act as signposts to the fact that everything in the Bible has a spiritual meaning. By this qualification Origen shows himself aware of the dangers of allegory in dissolving redemptive history into timeless myth. He had before him the spectre of gnostic exegesis, presupposing a radical discontinuity between the plane of history and the divine realm so that there can be no contact. He complains that the heretics go beyond scripture and regard the written letter as pernicious while claiming that their own esoteric doctrines are the life-giving spirit. Against them he quotes St. Paul's warning to the Corinthians that they must learn 'not to go beyond that which is written'. The Bible is an indispensable rung in the ladder of ascent, and remains so throughout this mortal life.[62] It is true that Origen looks forward to a comprehension of the gospel in the life of the world to come which will transcend the New Testament revelation just as the new covenant transcended the old.[63]

The same attitude emerges in Origen's remarks about the Church and its worship. The synaxis, the reading of scripture, and the common prayers belong to this present age, in which we see through a glass, darkly. The vision may often be dim, but at least it is only by

these means that we see anything at all. And Origen
has severe words to say of some contemporary heretics
who, on the ground that the true religion of the gospel
is solely spiritual and purely inward, separated from
the visible Church and rejected the observance of the
outward sacraments of baptism and eucharist.[64] Nevertheless, the only true apostolic succession is that seen in
the lives of the saints. The mystical language of Platonism combined with St. Paul's words about the superiority
of spirit to letter to convince Origen that spiritual power
is superior to ecclesiastical office.[65] In prayer the soul
is elevated above earthly matter and contemplates God
alone, looking into that mirror of the soul which reflects
the glory of the Lord and is transformed as the light of
the glory of God is stamped upon it.[66] The inward mind
is the correlate of God, and it is in the mind, not in the
body, that we are to find the image of God in man,[67]
which is the 'affinity' to God of which the Platonists
speak.

The Platonic idea of the relation between spirit and
matter was capable of being interpreted either in an
optimistic or in a pessimistic way. It could be construed
to mean that the visible world mirrors the glory of the
supra-sensible world. It could also be taken (as by the
Gnostics) to justify a radical rejection of the material
order as an accidental smudge, resulting from a mistake.
The fall of souls to incarceration in bodies is not a doctrine easily compatible with a high optimism concerning
the visible order, and this pessimism is much accentuated when joined with a belief in world-cycles

determined by destiny and the stars and in the transmigration of souls from body to body in successive lives.
Some of the Gnostics, such as Basilides,[68] had incorporated these beliefs in their systems. The critics of Origen
in the fourth century and later accused him of similar
fantasies. Jerome accuses Origen of believing that the
soul can even descend to animals and plants.[69] It was
an old charge, current even during the third century.
Pamphilus's *Apology for Origen* takes up the point, re-
marking that Origen's critics commonly fail to notice
that often Origen states a case without identifying himself with it and may even be stating the case for the view
he himself rejects.[70] The fact that Pamphilus thought
an apology needed shows that even as early as 300
critics were suspecting Origen of teaching the transmigration of souls. The recently discovered minutes of
a church council in Arabia, at which Origen was invited
as a theological expert to refute the heresy of a local
bishop named Heraclides and to explain the doctrine
of the soul, give a vivid picture of the suspicions with
which his Platonizing doctrine of the immortality of
souls was being greeted, even during his lifetime.[71]

Delicate questions are raised at this point. Origen's
doctrine of the nature and destiny of the soul is not
stated with a strong desire to draw a thick line of de-
marcation between the Platonic and the Biblical views.[72]
He takes the language of Genesis about the image of
God in man to justify the cautious use of Platonic terms
concerning the soul's 'natural affinity' for God.[73] Likewise he can speak of the Fall as the soul 'losing its wings',

echoing the *Phaedrus*,[74] and of soul as standing halfway between matter and spirit (a Platonist would have said *nous*).[75] Again, that souls pre-exist their life in this body seems to Origen to be a certainty. He thinks it absolutely necessary to any persuasive theodicy[76]—and the inequalities and apparent injustices of this present life were one of the most potent arguments of the Gnostics he wishes to combat.[77] The pre-existence of souls Origen finds in scripture in the text that John the Baptist leapt in his mother's womb.[78] In any event, the doctrine seemed self-evidently preferable to the all too materialistic doctrine of the traducianists that the soul is derived with the body from the parental seed and is transmitted by the lowly process of reproduction, or to the seemingly fussy creationist notion that every time a human couple casually conceive a child, God is put to the pains of sending a soul to inhabit the embryo.[79] But the first motive is always the most powerful: like Plato himself in the *Republic*,[80] Origen must assert the pre-existence of souls because he must explain the diversity of human fortune in this world as a consequence of choices freely made by souls before their incarnation here.

Origen makes next to no serious use of the Platonic doctrine that learning is recollection and reminiscence.[81] But the myth of transmigration was a graver matter. Reincarnation implied fatalistic conceptions of the soul's destiny, and is explicitly rejected in the *contra Celsum*.[82] Even if Origen felt bound to concede that reincarnation is 'a very plausible opinion',[83] yet he sharply attacks

Plato's notion that the rational soul, made in the image of God, can sink so low as to be imprisoned in an animal body[84]—a doctrine which the Platonists defended on the ground that all souls are of one essence and form.[85] But it is noteworthy that Origen does not offer a reasoned criticism of the notion that souls may be reincarnate in human bodies.

The problem is obviously bound up with that of the eternity of the world, a question which was the subject of lively debate in the contemporary Platonic schools. In whatever way the first chapter of Genesis was allegorized, a Christian theologian was likely to insist that at least the created order is contingent and finite, and that it moves from a beginning to an end which rests in the will of the Creator. The generally accepted theology of paganism, as we find it in men like Celsus and Porphyry, is different in its emphasis. To them the world is an unending cycle, controlled by the stars and planets, with its course punctuated by floods and conflagrations. These disasters arise when there is an excess of the elements of either water or fire. The theory had the advantage that it not only made room for the ancient myths of the flood of Deucalion and the conflagration of Phaethon but also met the serious objection: if the world is eternal, why do the records of civilization go back such a short way? The answer to this question was that they had been destroyed (except in Egypt which, according to the *Timaeus*, was specially exempt from cosmic catastrophes and therefore possessed records going back many millennia).[86]

Jews and Christians before Origen had tried to come to terms with this belief by discovering a cosmic flood and conflagration in the stories of Noah and of the cities of the plain.[87] Origen makes no use of this notion, and sees no difficulty in accepting from Genesis the simple view that the visible world was created 'less than six thousand years ago'.[88] He regarded the whole conception of an unending world rolling on its way to alternating catastrophes as altogether too deterministic, and preferred to see the cycle of creation, fall, and redemption as dependent exclusively upon the good providence of God and the freedom of the rational creature originally made in God's image. It is part of the paradox of Origen's speculations that, although aggressively rejecting the Platonic doctrine of an endless cyclic world, he himself taught in effect a doctrine which, despite its different foundation, looked almost identical. For example, he freely and repeatedly makes his own the conventional Platonic argument that the world must be without beginning or end, because the Immutable Creator can never be conceived of as inactive.[89] But in Origen's cosmology it is the higher spiritual world that is coeternal with the Creator, and not this inferior material world.

One logical argument used by Origen against the eternity of the world is worth noticing, since it came to have a future. In the *de Principiis* and in the commentary on St. Matthew he argues that the infinite or unending is unknowable; yet it is part of the definition of God that he knows all things concerning the created world: therefore, Origen concludes, the world is knowable and in consequence necessarily finite with both beginning and end.[90] The exponents of transmigration were able to turn the argument against the Christians by saying that, if the events in the world are finite, it follows from the finitude of the world which is also the object of God's unending and eternal care that there must be an endless repetition of events. Their number cannot be infinite. Yet the creation of an eternal Creator must be. This argument probably occurred in Porphyry's commentary on the *Timaeus*, and by the time of the emperor Julian has become a regular part of the anti-Christian arsenal.[91] Augustine answers it by saying that divine knowledge of the finite need not be finite, and that God comprehends the incomprehensible with an incomprehensible comprehension.[92] Exchanges continued between pagan and Christian on this subject as late as the sixth century, when Origen's argument is restated by Aeneas of Gaza and John Philoponus of Alexandria and is attacked by Simplicius.[93] The logic of an argument about the incomprehensible is necessarily obscure, but Origen was working with propositions that had the force of axioms for his Platonist contemporaries. It is ironic that his sophisticated argument for a finite creation was taken by Theophilus of Alexandria and by Justinian to be an argument against ascribing unlimited power to God and therefore additional evidence of his blasphemy.[94]

If these arguments are dead, Origen's universalism is not. It is essential to a just view of Origen's doctrine to recognize that there is no particle of sentimentality in his make-up. His case always rests on the creative goodness of God as the ground of redemption. Therefore, Christ's atoning work remains in an important sense incomplete until every soul made in his image has been restored to communion with God.[95] And so long as the creature remains rational and free, there is always the possibility of conversion.[96] God has made none evil. Even if many have become so sinful that evil has become second nature, yet for the divine Word to change evil that has become deeply ingrained is 'not only not impossible but is not even very difficult, if only a man admits that he must trust himself to God'. To say that it is intrinsically impossible for a really evil being to be converted is not merely to surrender the entire position to Gnosticism, but also to say that such a person has lost reason. It is to find fault with the Creator, not with him, since he is no longer responsible.[97] The redeemed do not move to their destiny in God by a natural and inevitable process. The steps to heaven are a staircase to be climbed, not an escalator; and predestination is always interpreted by Origen (as by most of the Greek Fathers) in terms of foreseen merits.[98] Therefore, Origen does not affirm universal salvation as something we can all comfortably take for granted, and it is more his hope than his assured certitude. In one passage in his commentary on St. Matthew he remarks that according to the Stoics the end of the world comes by a natural process in which everything is absorbed in fire, whereas scripture ascribes the coming of the end to the will and providence of God in judgement.[99]

Perhaps it is this insistence on freedom in God which most deeply marks Origen's theology with a Biblical stamp. We have seen that the main weight of Celsus's attack falls upon the Biblical doctrine of God. For Celsus there is an unbridgeable gulf between the God who is beyond being and this world of change and decay. He scorns the 'personalism' of Biblical faith, and opposes to the Christian view a determinism which thinks of providence as simply the natural process at work. The nerve-centre of the debate between Origen and Celsus lies in the possibility of revelation in history: can there be grace? To Celsus the Christian doctrine means that God's freedom is arbitrary and capricious. Origen rejects this as a crude misunderstanding and misrepresentation. For him the ultimate question is whether God is goodness and love: if so, he cares for his creation and his goodness is the principle we are to discern throughout experience.

In judging the system of Origen as a whole it is important to remember that some of the most characteristic features of 'Origenism' are not his personal invention, but go back behind him to Clement and to Philo. The idea, which caused such offence in the sixth century, that souls fell from the divine realm as a result of a satiety, and the notion that the material world is posterior to spirit, are both ideas that are already found in Philo.[100] It is also important to remember that the theses associated with Origen's name in the controversy of the time of Justinian, which led to condemnation at the General Council of 553, are more due to the development of the speculative and mystical side of Origen at the hands of Evagrius in the fourth century than to the work of Origen himself. But the question whether Origen should be judged orthodox or not is not one that can be settled merely by demonstrating that Justinian was unfair or that Jerome was not above the time-honoured controversial technique of quoting against Origen his statement of the view which he was engaged in refuting. Origen is not vindicated by arguments which only go to show that Koetschau's Berlin corpus edition of the *de Principiis* is open to serious criticism for its excessive scepticism towards Rufinus and excessive credulity towards Origen's enemies.

Nor again can Origen be proved to be heretical by picking out isolated points and particular flights of speculation. He was writing at a time when he had neither the Nicene Creed nor the Chalcedonian definition to assist or to restrict him. The theologians of the fourth and fifth centuries were aware that early Christian writers had expressed themselves more loosely than later divinity could allow, and in most cases were prepared to exercise charity in interpretation. But on one such passage in Origen Epiphanius makes the revealing comment 'Such language would be excusable in anyone else'.[101] The comment exposes the nerve of the matter. Had Origen heretical intentions? For in a writer of heretical intentions even the most orthodox-sounding passages are full of danger and should be distrusted as a diabolical snare.[102] Origen himself teaches that one must not do right if it is the devil who tempts one to do it.[103] Therefore merely to enumerate strictly orthodox passages in his writings will not suffice to save him. Nor is it enough to point to the acceptance that his sermons achieved in the monasteries of the west or to the direct influence that he can be shown to have exercised upon the highest spirituality of medieval Christendom.[104] Even so sympathetic a reader as Basil of Caesarea, who owed Origen more than he himself knew, was sufficiently moved by Epiphanius's onslaught to declare that Origen's real opinions were heretical and that orthodox passages in his works are only the consequence of his unconscious respect for Church tradition.[105]

If the meaning of orthodoxy is to wish to believe as the Church believes, then there can be virtually no hesitation in pronouncing Origen orthodox. He has a passionate sense of the Church as a divinely ordained society and of the normative character of its belief and practice for all believers. The model of Christ himself is always before his eyes. So sensitive is he to the charge of adulterating Christianity with Platonism that his attitude to Plato and the great philosophers becomes prickly and even aggressively rude. He wanted to be a Christian, not a Platonist. Yet Platonism was inside him, *malgré lui*, absorbed into the very axioms and presuppositions of his thinking. Moreover, this penetration of his thought by Platonism is no merely external veneer of apologetic. Platonic ways of thinking about God and the soul are necessary to him if he is to give an intelligible account of his Christian beliefs.

Orthodoxy is a word that suggests clear-cut and

absolute lines of division. It begins to look different if we ask whether some theologians may be more orthodox than others, whether there are degrees of understanding, whether, if we all see through a glass, darkly, some may be able to see a little more clearly than others. The question is one formulated by Origen himself when he discusses the status of Christians who believe all the creed except for one article such as the Virgin Birth.[106] Origen saw that the formal credal propositions have to be stated in an unqualified and dogmatic form. But the reasons and the underlying pattern beneath these affirmations are for him matters of cautious investigation and speculative inquiry. Here there is great danger in over-confidence. In advanced matters of theology, he once remarks, absolute confidence is possible only for two classes of people, saints and idiots.[107]

Erasmus wrote once that he learned more of Christian philosophy from one page of Origen than from ten pages of Augustine.[108] He tended to see in Origen a reflection of his own humanist face. It would be difficult and unnecessary to deny the humanism of Origen's scholarship and philosophical temper. At the same time a just view of him must declare that there is more in him that is illiberal, world-denying, and ascetic. And if he remains a perennially enigmatic and embarrassing figure in the history of Christian thought, this is perhaps most due to the fact that we tend to begin the study of Origen by asking whether or not he is orthodox, and find that in the process we are continually driven back to the prior question: what is the essence of orthodoxy?

NOTES

(1) Tertullian, *de Praescr.* 7; *Apol.* 46. There is a direct echo in Jerome, *Ep.* 22. 29.

(2) Tertullian, *de Carne Christi* 5. For Justin see below p. 130, n. 50.

(3) For Tertullian's mind and culture see above all J. H. Waszink's encyclopaedic commentary on his *de Anima* (Amsterdam, 1947). For a short study of his attitude to philosophy cf. A. Labhard, 'Tertullien et la philosophie ou la recherche d'une position pure', *Museum Helveticum* vii (1950), 159–80.

(4) Tertullian, *de Testimonio Animae.* (See Waszink's notes on *de Anima* 41.) There is a striking parallel in Proclus, *in Tim.* I. 369, 20, Diehl.

(5) The closest allusion is *Ap.* i. 61. 4 'Christ said, Unless you are born again, you shall not enter the kingdom of heaven'; but it is not an exact citation of John iii and, if it stood alone, could readily be explained as independent use of floating tradition associated with baptism and catechism. The positive case rests on the cumulative effect of many passing phrases, e.g. 'the only begotten of the Father' (*Dial.* 105. 1), 'the water of life' (14. 1; 114. 4), 'fount of living water' (69. 6), Christ healing those 'maimed from birth' (69. 6), the serpent in the wilderness as a type of redemption (91, 94, 112, 131, *Ap.* i. 60. 2–3), and John the Baptist's explicit denial that he is the Christ, as in John i. 20 (*Dial.* 88. 7), though this might equally well come from Acts xiii. 25. Justin's knowledge of the fourth gospel (the fullest statement of the case for this remains Zahn's *Geschichte des N. T. Kanons* i (Erlangen, 1888), 516–34) was sharply denied by E. Schwartz in *Nachr. d. Götting. Akad.* (1908), pp. 142 ff., and is regarded as 'more than doubtful' by W. Schneemelcher in his fine introduction to the new edition of Hennecke, *Neutestamentliche Apokryphen* i (Tübingen, 1959), 10 (= Eng. tr., ed. R. McL. Wilson, p. 32). I should prefer to say 'less than certain

but still the most probable and simple hypothesis'. The absence of Johannine influence on the fundamental structure of Justin's theology does not seem a serious difficulty. The apartness of the fourth gospel would tend to be much accentuated if, as *Ap*. i. 16. 9–12 and 33. 5 suggest, Justin used a current synoptic gospel-harmony to which, before Tatian's Diatessaron, St. John had not yet been added. For argument that Justin may well have had such a harmony see W. Sanday, *The Gospels in the Second Century* (London, 1876), pp. 91–136; E. Lippelt, *Quae fuerint Justini Martyris Apomnemoneumata* (Halle, 1901); H. Köster, *Synoptische Überlieferung bei den aspostolischen Vätern = T.U.* 65 (1957), pp. 89 ff.; H. F. D. Sparks in *JTS* N.S. xiv (1963), 465. I do not think the observations about Justin's method of quotation by E. R. Buckley in *JTS* xxxvi (1935), 173–6, incompatible with this conclusion.

In passing, attention may be drawn to É. de Strycker's argument that the case for affirming Justin's knowledge of the *Protevangelium of James* is too weak to stand (*La forme la plus ancienne du Protévangile de Jacques* (Louvain, 1961), pp. 414–17).

(6) See the thoughtful remarks of H. von Campenhausen, *Tradition und Leben* (Tübingen, 1960), pp. 17–47.

(7) Plutarch, *Qu. Conv.* iv. 6, 671–2; Tacitus, *Hist.* v. 4. If W. M. Calder's interpretation is correct (*Journ. Hell. Stud.* xxxi (1911), 196), the identification of the Jewish God with Dionysus also appears in a dedicatory inscription Ἰνῷ Διονύσῳ from north of Iconium. By equating Sabaoth and Sabazius it might be asserted that the Jews worshipped the Phrygian and Thracian deity Zeus Sabazius (Valerius Maximus, i. 3. 2). Egyptians could identify the God of the Jews with Osiris (Lydus, *de Mensibus* iv. 53). The Jewish claim that they worshipped the supreme power led Varro to identify their God with Jupiter (Augustine, *de Cons. Evang.* i. 30), though he also knew that they called him Iao (Lydus, loc. cit.). The idea that the Jewish God has a specific name creates some embarrassment for hellenized writers like Philo for whom the namelessness of God is essential to belief in transcendence (*Mut. Nom.* 11 ff., etc.). Hellenizing Jews could simply call their deity 'the Most High' (*Hypsistos*): e.g. Philo, *Leg.* 278, and especially Celsus in Origen's *c. Cels.* i. 23–24 and v. 41 ('Most High or Adonai or Heavenly One or Sabaoth or whatever name they (i.e. the Jews)

like to give this universe'). But they do not seem to have thought of *Hypsistos* as a proper name. In fourth-century Asia Minor the worship of 'Hypsistos' or 'Pantokrator' had a following consisting, it seems, partly of hellenized Jews and partly of Gentiles attracted to hellenized Judaism, like Gregory Nazianzen's father (Greg. Naz. *Or.* 18. 5; Epiphanius, *Panar.* 80. 1. 4 f.); and perhaps for them *Hypsistos* virtually became a cultic title. The occurrence of the epithet in Jewish inscriptions at Delos and the Crimea (J. B. Frey, *Corpus Inscr. Iud.* i. 690, 725, 727–30; see also 78*, p. 577) is not in itself evidence of syncretism, though no doubt the Jews in these places were very liberal in their assimilation to the Greeks around them. Since Schürer's paper (*Sitzungsber. Berlin Akad.* (1897), pp. 200–25) the Crimean inscriptions have been much discussed, opinion being divided whether the worshippers were hellenizing Jews (so Schürer) or judaizing Gentiles (so E. R. Goodenough in *Jewish Quarterly Review*, N.S. xlvii (1956–7), 211–43). A convenient summary of the essential evidence will be found in A. B. Cook's *Zeus* ii (Cambridge, 1925), 883 f. It is noteworthy that despite the Septuagintal usage of *Hypsistos* for God, this epithet is not used as a proper name in invocations preserved in the magical papyri. No doubt the prime intention behind its use was precisely to avoid a proper name. Cf. A. D. Nock, *H.T.R.* 29 (1936), pp. 55–69.

(8) Col. ii. 8.

(9) *Enn.* ii. 9, discussed by Carl Schmidt, *Plotins Stellung zum Gnostizismus und kirchlichen Christentum = T.U.* 20, 4 (1901), and by H.-C. Puech in *Entretiens Hardt* v (1960), 159–90. Cf. also R. Harder, *Kleine Schriften* (1960), pp. 296–302.

(10) In time Justin came to receive the credit for the authorship of many additional works (including, e.g., the epistle to Diognetus and some 'Antiochene' works like the *Expositio rectae fidei* now known to be the work of Theodoret). The growth of the pseudo-Justin corpus seems to have been a process that began comparatively early, even before Eusebius in the fourth century. Most of the fragments ascribed to him in Byzantine writers have no claim to be accepted as authentic, and the spurious works loom large in Photius's notice (*Bibl.* 125). An exception may perhaps be made in favour of the extracts from a work on the resurrection cited as Justin's in the *Sacra Parallela* of John of Damascus; these fragments could have

been written by Justin, though their theology is less sophisticated than his, and must be classified as doubtful rather than as certainly spurious. Undisputed are the three short fragments preserved by Irenaeus (*adv. Haer.* iv. 6. 2; v. 26. 3) and Tatian (*Or.* 18); and there is no good reason to question that preserved by Methodius (*de Resurr.* ii. 18. 9, the Greek being preserved by Photius, *Bibl.* 234). Unhappily none of these four fragments materially adds to the comprehension of Justin's thought. For brief discussion and translations of the fragments of Justin, authentic and spurious (but excluding the work on the resurrection), see R. M. Grant in *Biblical and Patristic Studies in Memory of R. P. Casey* (Freiburg, 1963), pp. 182–8. It should be emphasized that the condition of the Greek text of the *Dialogue* and *Apologies* transmitted by the Paris codex (Paris. gr. 450) is bad and that there is still no adequate critical edition. The Acts of Justin's martyrdom, evidently based on contemporary record of the proceedings and free of hagiographical embroidery, have a different and substantially superior manuscript tradition.

It may be noted also that the western martyrologies long ignored Justin; his present place in the Roman martyrology is due to the initiative of Florus of Lyons in the ninth century, who put him on 13 April because of his association with Carpus and Agathonice in Eusebius, *H.E.* iv. 15. 48. (Leo XIII transferred him to 14 April.) The Greek commemoration on 1 June is much older than any western celebration of the Roman martyr. Nothing of Justin passed into Latin translation before 1554, when a version was made from Stephanus' *editio princeps* of 1551.

(11) See below, p. 128, n. 26.

(12) *Ap.* i. 54.

(13) *Ap.* i. 58. 3.

(14) *Ap.* i. 24 and 29. 4. These orgies were censured as much by Celsus as by Christian writers: cf. references in my translation of Origen, *c. Cels.* iii. 36.

(15) *Ap.* ii. 10. 3; 13. 3; cf. i. 4. 8.

(16) *Ap.* i. 43; ii. 7.

(17) *Ap.* ii. 7; cf. i. 20. For the identification of Noah and Deucalion see Philo, *Praem.* 23; Theophilus, *ad Autol.* iii. 19; Origen, *c. Cels.*

iv. 11 and 41. Justin may have read some of Philo's tracts, since there are a number of correspondences and contacts, not all of which are mere commonplaces shared with other writers, but his knowledge cannot be affirmed as a certainty. Cf. my remarks in *Bulletin of the John Rylands Library* 47 (1965), 296 f.

(18) *Ap.* ii. 13. 2 and the implications of *Dial.* 2–5. On Plato in second-century apologetic there is a good discussion in J. Daniélou, *Message évangélique et culture hellénistique* (Paris, 1961), pp. 103–22.

(19) *Ap.* i. 5; ii. 10. It is noteworthy that Justin, unlike Origen (*c. Cels.* v. 43; vi. 4; vii. 42 ff.), does not accuse Plato and Socrates of failing to break with polytheism. On the evaluation of Socrates in the early Church there is a well-known lecture by Harnack (*Reden und Aufsätze* I. i (Giessen, 1904), 29 ff.), a detailed study by E. Benz in *Z.N.W.* 43 (1950–1), 195–223, and a more general survey by E. Fascher in *Z.N.W.* 45 (1954), 1–41.

(20) Unbegotten and impassible: *Ap.* i. 25. 2, cf. 49. 5; 53. 2; ii. 12. 4; *Dial.* 5. 4. Nameless: *Ap.* i. 61. 11; 63. 1; ii. 6. 1; 12. 4.

(21) *Ap.* i. 20. 4. Note Justin's review of the exegesis of the *Timaeus* (*Dial.* 5) where he insists that creation is a temporal act (as some contemporary Platonists were saying). The Septuagint translation of Gen. i. 2 as 'invisible and unformed' suggested correspondence with *Timaeus* 51 A, 'invisible and shapeless'.

(22) *Ap.* i. 10. 2; 59. 1; ii. 6. 3.

(23) Kinship to God: *Dial.* 4. 2. Free will of angels and men: *Dial.* 88. 5; 102. 4; 140. 4; 141. 1; *Ap.* ii. 7. 5; cf. i. 10. 4 and 28. 3 on faith as a moral choice. Punishment hereafter: *Ap.* i. 44 (taken by Plato from Moses).

(24) *Dial.* 4–6.

(25) *Ap.* ii. 10. 6. On the interpretation of *Tim.* 28 c in the Platonic tradition cf. A. D. Nock in *Vigiliae Christianae* xvi (1962), 79–86. The text was part of the tradition of Platonic anthologies, and so what every schoolboy knew. For a collection of references see A. S. Pease's commentary on Cicero, *de Natura Deorum* i. 12. 30. Justin has 'unsafe' for Plato's 'impossible', a variant shared with the contemporary Platonist Albinus and Josephus (*c. Ap.* ii. 224); cf. Daniélou, op. cit., p. 104.

(26) Caricatures of the incarnation and birth of Jesus: *Dial.* 69–70;

78. 6; *Ap.* i. 22–23 and 54; of baptism and of bare feet at exorcism: *Ap.* i. 62; the Mithraic eucharist: *Ap.* i. 66. Images of Kore beside springs (*Ap.* i. 64) were evoked by Gen. i. 2 (the spirit moving on the waters). (An illuminating commentary on this last suggestion of Justin is provided by Numenius of Apamea's comments on the same text of Genesis, cited by Porphyry, *de Antro Nympharum* 10. Probably Justin knows of some previous syncretistic exposition of Genesis i, perhaps of gnostic origin. This seems more likely than the far-fetched hypothesis that Justin was remembering from his Samaritan childhood the cult of goddesses at springs in Syria and Palestine—the suggestion of Reitzenstein, *Die Vorgeschichte der christlichen Taufe* (1929), p. 35.) On the other hand, Justin will not allow that cruciform shapes in the natural order can have been inspired by the devils, since to them the mystery of the crucifixion was incomprehensible (*Ap.* i. 55, cf. 1 Cor. ii. 8 f.; Ign. *Eph.* 19).

(27) Cicero, *de Finibus* v. 29. 87; Plutarch, *de Iside* 10, 354 E; Diogenes Laertius iii. 6; Philostratus, *Vita Apollonii* i. 2; Jerome, *Ep.* 53. 1, etc.

(28) Origen, *c. Cels.* iv. 39. The fact that in the *Timaeus* Solon learns of cosmic floods from an Egyptian priest provided invaluable support for this theory, developed by a number of writers.

(29) Aug. *de Civ. Dei*, viii. 11, withdrawing his earlier acceptance of this view on the authority of Ambrose (*de Doctr. Chr.* ii. 28. 43).

(30) For example, the anonymous life of Plato summarized by Photius, *Bibl.* 249; Augustine, *de Doctr. Chr.* ii. 28. 43.

(31) Clem. Al. *Strom.* i. 150. 4. The extant fragments of Numenius give no clear evidence that he had read Philo.

(32) Eusebius of Caesarea, *P.E.* xi. 19. 1.

(33) *Ap.* i. 60.

(34) *Dial.* 55 ff.

(35) *Dial.* 60. 2; cf. 127. 2. There are several anticipations in Philo: *V.Mos.* i. 66; *Som.* i. 69, 231 f.; *Fug.* 141; *Mut. Nom.* 134; *Spec. Leg.* i. 329, etc.

(36) See especially C. C. Richardson, *The Doctrine of the Trinity* (New York and Nashville, 1958).

(37) *Ap*. i. 46.

(38) *Ap*. ii. 8. 1–3; 10. 8; 13.

(39) *Ap*. i. 55. Cf. J. E. B. Mayor on Tert. *Apol*. 16.

(40) *Ap*. i. 14. 5.

(41) *Dial*. 142. 3; cf. 3. 4.

(42) *Ap*. i. 12. 7; ii. 2. 13; 9. 4.

(43) *Dial*. 93.

(44) e.g. *Dial*. 125. 3 f. Note Justin's polemic against adoptianism in 88. 2 f. and 8 (Christ did not become Son of God but was so from birth, as the story of the Magi's homage shows; the divine word at his baptism, 'This day have I begotten thee', means that thenceforth men began to realize who he was).

(45) *Ap*. ii. 10. The argument is very frequent in early Christian writers; it already had currency in Jewish apologetic in aid of the claims of Moses (Josephus, *c. Apion*. ii. 169).

(46) *Dial*. 7; 48. 3.

(47) *Ap*. ii. 10. 8.

(48) Miracles: *Ap*. i. 30; *Dial*. 11. 4; 69. Prophecy: *Ap*. i. 30 ff. and throughout the Dialogue. Extension to all races: *Ap*. i. 39 and 53; *Dial*. 83. 4; 91. 3; 117. 5; 121. 1. Cf. 110. 4 (blood of the martyrs the seed of the Church).

(49) 'The Christians alone offer proof': *Ap*. i. 20. 3; 54. 1; 58. 2. Meeting the charge that Christians believe on blind faith, Justin retorts that it is the pagans who are blind and prejudiced inasmuch as they refuse Christianity a free and open examination (like the Cynic Crescens in Rome, *Ap*. ii. 3), taking their opinion of Christianity on vulgar hearsay without any serious inquiry (*Ap*. i. 11. 1) and preferring custom to truth (*Ap*. i. 2; 12. 6 and 11; 53. 12; 57. 1). Justin formally protests that he does not ask anyone to believe anything without the fullest scrutiny (*Ap*. i. 2; *Dial*. 68. 2).

(50) *Ap*. i. 53. 2. Justin insists on the 'paradoxes' of Christianity (*Dial*. 38. 2; 49. 6; 68. 1–2). Cf. his anti-docetic emphasis, *Dial*. 98. 1; 99. 2; 103. 8.

(51) *Dial*. 80; 118. 2; 138. 3; 139. 4–5. Justin is aware of some who

deny this millennial hope but describes them as 'unorthodox'. This censure stands in noteworthy contrast to his only mildly disapproving language about some Christians who, while believing that Jesus is Christ, do not accept the Virgin Birth (*Dial.* 48. 4). Irenaeus (*adv. Haer.* v. 33–36) so sharply confutes would-be orthodox Christians who take the millenarian texts symbolically, that these chapters became embarrassing and were omitted in the Arundel manuscript and its dependent copies.

(52) In Clement there is no disavowal or even discussion of millennial dreams, but his symbolist interpretation of the twelve gates of the heavenly city (*Pd.* ii. 119) leaves no doubt about his view. Origen's few allusions (*de Princ.* ii. 11. 2; *Comm. in Cant. Cantic.* prol., p. 66 Baehrens; *Comm. in Matt.* xvii. 35; *de Orat.* xxvii. 13, 'the much debated millennium'; cf. the critique in Methodius, *de Creatis*, p. 499 Bonwetsch = Photius, *cod.* 235) are decisively against any literal exegesis.

(53) This thesis is important for Justin because it makes possible his answer to the question 'if the coming of Christ was as clearly predicted by the prophets as you say, why have most Jews failed to believe him?' Justin's answer is the blinding effect of custom and conservatism (*Dial.* 38–39; 123. 6; 125. 5, etc.). He remains clear that the salvation of the Jews is God's eternal will (*Dial.* 92. 6), and allows that those who faithfully keep the Mosaic law, even though observing many needless ceremonies, may indeed be saved; but they must not persecute Christ's disciples or anathematize him in the synagogue service (*Dial.* 45).

(54) *Dial.* 80. 2; 120. 6; 125. 1.

(55) A corrective to the scornful disparagement of Geffcken (*Zwei griechische Apologeten* (Leipzig, 1907), pp. 98–104) is provided by A. Puech, *Les Apologistes grecs* (Paris, 1912), and by the examination of Justin's relation to contemporary Platonism by Carl Andresen, *Z.N.W.* 44 (1952–3), 157–95. See also Andresen's book, *Logos und Nomos* (Berlin, 1955), pp. 312–44, and, on the Platonism of the opening of the Dialogue, W. Schmid in *Hermeneia: Festschrift O. Regenbogen* (Heidelberg, 1952), pp. 163–82. The contacts between Justin and Stoicism may be extracted from the useful compendium of M. Spanneut, *Le Stoïcisme des Pères de l'Église* (Paris, 1957). For

Justin's thought as a whole see E. R. Goodenough, *The Theology of Justin Martyr* (Jena, 1923), and a notable article by G. Bardy in *Dict. Théol. Cath.* viii (1924–5), 2228–2277. I have discussed some aspects of Justin's achievement in *Bulletin of the John Rylands Library* for March 1965, vol. 47, pp. 275–297.

(56) Lucian's fullest statement is his *Hermotimus*, but the view is frequently expressed in his writings (e.g. *Piscator* 6, *Menippus* 3 ff., etc.). He remarks that his sceptical objections would have no force against one who had really examined all the different schools (*Hermot.* 46). Justin's autobiographical account (*Dial.* 2) of his career going the round of various teachers, Stoic, Peripatetic, Pythagorean, and Platonist, is probably intended as an implicit answer to the kind of criticism that Lucian offers. In the trial before the prefect Rusticus Justin makes the same point by implication when he says, 'I have tried to get to know all doctrines, but I have given my assent to the true doctrines of the Christians' (*Acta S. Justini* 2). In Lucian the sceptic extracts from Hermotimus the admission that he became a Stoic merely because most people were doing so (*Hermot.* 16); this superior popularity of Stoic teachers would explain why Justin went to a Stoic first. The absence of an Epicurean from Justin's catalogue needs no explaining. He accepts the popular view of Epicurus as an amoral hedonist (*Ap.* ii. 7. 3; 12. 5; 15. 3), attested in Platonists like Maximus of Tyre. Justin's Pythagorean demanded preparation; cf. Taurus in Gellius, *N.A.* i. 9. 8 f.

(57) Numenius's fragments are collected by E. A. Leemans, *Studie over den wijsgeer Numenius van Apamea met Uitgave der Fragmenten* (Mémoires de l'Acad. roy. de Belgique, Classe des lettres, 37. 2, 1937). See also H.-C. Puech, 'Numenius d'Apamée et les théologies orientales au second siècle', in *Mélanges Bidez* (Brussels, 1934), pp. 745 ff.; E. R. Dodds, 'Numenius and Ammonius', *Entretiens sur l'antiquité classique* v (1960), 1–61; R. Beutler, *PW. Suppl.* vii. 664.

(58) For a recent study of the Fathers along this line see C. Tresmontant, *La Métaphysique du Christianisme et la naissance de la philosophie chrétienne* (Paris, 1961), well criticized by R. F. Refoulé, *Rev. de l'hist. des religions* 163 (1963), 11–52.

(59) The case for thinking that Celsus has Justin specifically in view, proposed by some nineteenth-century scholars such as Pela-

gaud, has been argued in close detail by Carl Andresen, *Logos und Nomos* (1955), chiefly on the ground that Celsus's 'plagiarism' argument is in logical structure identical with Justin's and adopts the same techniques. Just as Justin thinks pagan notions arise from misunderstood texts of scripture, so Celsus thinks Christian ideas arise from misunderstood texts of Plato. More speculatively Andresen points to detailed contacts. Both invoke Plato (?), *Ep*. 2, 312 DE (*Ap*. i. 60. 6 f.; Celsus vi. 18); both know of parallels between Christianity and Mithraism (*Ap*. i. 66. 4; Celsus vi. 22 f.); Justin treats transmigration as a misunderstanding of the Resurrection (*Ap*. i. 19. 4), an argument which Celsus neatly reverses (vii. 32). Celsus devotes much labour to controverting the arguments from miracle (i. 28 ff. on virgin birth; i. 68; ii. 30, 48 ff., 55 ff. on resurrection) and from fulfilled prophecy (i. 50; iv. 33; v. 6; vi. 81; vii. 11 f., 18; viii. 48), which are both prominent in Justin (above, p. 130, n. 48). H knows (iii. 22 ff.) of Christian criticism of Greek heroes; cf. Justin, *Ap*. i. 21 and 54.

Further affinities are enumerated by A. D. Nock in his review of Andresen in *JTS* N.s. vii (1956), 316 n. 4; Celsus (ii. 55; iii. 22) criticizes the character of witnesses to the Resurrection much as Justin criticizes witnesses to the ascent of deified emperors (*Ap*. i. 21. 3); Celsus's denial of the possibility of a radical change of character (iii. 65) could reply to Justin, *Ap*. i. 14. Celsus's attacks on hell (iii. 16; iv. 10; viii. 48) recall Justin's references (*Ap*. i. 12, 18, etc.). His scorn of anthropocentrism (iv. 74 ff.) directly touches Justin (*Ap*. i. 10. 2; ii. 5. 2; *Dial*. 5. 2; 41. 1). Both Celsus (i. 67) and Trypho (*Dial*. 67) compare the Virgin Birth to the myth of Perseus (cf. *Ap*. i. 22). Perhaps Trypho's role in the Dialogue (see esp. his concessions, 10. 2; 56. 10; 67. 8) suggested to Celsus his much less cooperative Jewish interlocutor in *c. Cels*. i–ii.

To these we might add that Justin's (unorthodox) doctrine that Christ's blood was divine, not human (*Dial*. 54; 63. 2; 76. 2; *Ap*. i. 32. 9), recalls Celsus's jibe: 'Was Christ's blood ichor such as flows in the veins of the blessed gods?' (i. 66; ii. 36).

(60) Celsus vi. 15.

(61) vii. 58.

(62) vi. 16.

(63) vi. 19 f.; cf. vii. 28.

(64) vi. 12.

(65) vi. 16 and 12. Augustine meets the same contention (*de Doctr. Chr.* ii. 28. 43; *Ep.* 31. 8).

(66) i. 14. The dominant importance of this theme for Celsus was brought out in a stimulating paper by A. Wifstrand, 'Die wahre Lehre des Kelsos', *Bulletin de la Société royale des lettres de Lund*, 1941–2, 5. Wifstrand showed that his argument hangs on the theme of a gradual depravation through history of the primordial truth clearly apprehended by the most ancient races of mankind—'the Egyptians, Assyrians, Indians, Persians, Odrysians, Samothracians and Eleusinians' (Celsus i. 14).

A close parallel is found in Lucian's survey of the history of philosophy (*Fugitivi*) where the initial revelation was made to the Indians, Brahmans, Ethiopians, Egyptians, Chaldaeans, Magi, Scythians, and Thracians, but in Greece was corrupted by the sophists. Cf. also the account of the Jews' degeneration into superstition given by Strabo xvi. 2. 35–39. The idea that the first men 'were better than we and lived nearer the gods' is in Plato, *Philebus* 16 c. Philo (*Virt.* 79) claims that 'from the beginning' the whole Jewish nation was akin to God.

(67) The dissident, seditious spirit (viii. 1 and 49) is so ingrained that if everyone were to be converted the Christians would be quite at a loss (iii. 9).

(68) ii. 1, 4, 6; esp. iii. 5; v. 33, 41.

(69) iii. 5; iv. 31.

(70) i. 21–24; iv. 36; v. 41.

(71) i. 14 (the O.T. is tendentious pro-Jewish propaganda); iii. 1 (the dispute between Jews and Christians is a quarrel about futilities between parties whose absurdity is about equal); v. 6 (the Jews refuse to worship the heavenly bodies, yet they venerate the heaven and the angels); v. 14 (most Jews hold a crude doctrine of resurrection); v. 41 (the Jews' claim to unique favour is refuted by the fact that other races besides them practise circumcision and abstain from pigs—comparative religion makes everything relative—cf. i. 22 and vii. 62).

(72) v. 25–33. Cf. Plutarch, *Qu. Rom.* 83.

(73) iv. 14.

(74) i. 4.

(75) Specially significant are Celsus's concessions that Moses derived some part of his doctrine from the ancient tradition (i. 21), and that the Christian claims for special acts of divine revelation can be positively interpreted when they are brought within this framework of ideas (vii. 45).

(76) iv. 42.

(77) i. 19–20; iv. 11 and 79.

(78) iv. 65.

(79) vi. 1–vii. 58.

(80) i. 9.

(81) iii. 44–58.

(82) See i. 17, 27, 62 f. (the apostles, wicked tax-collectors, and sailors; cf. ii. 46); iii. 48 ff. (the stupid, slaves, women, children), iv. 42 (stories of O.T. patriarchs mere nursery stuff), 49–52 (pitiable and contemptible), 87 (crude and illiterate); v. 65 (vulgar and arrogant); vi. 1 ff. (yokels); vi. 14 (Christians flee headlong from the educated, but entrap illiterates), etc.

(83) For example, Harnack, *Die Mission und Ausbreitung des Christentums*⁴ (Leipzig, 1924), p. 374; W. Völker, *Das Bild vom nichtgnostischen Christentum bei Celsus* (Halle, 1928), pp. 87–88.

(84) Above, p. 133, n. 59.

(85) ii. 31 (Logos); iii. 43 (tomb of Zeus).

(86) i. 17; iv. 38; 48–51; 89.

(87) i. 9; vi. 11–12.

(88) v. 14.

(89) vi. 11.

(90) iii. 1 ff.; cf. v. 52 (Jesus from the same God); 61 (some of them will agree that they have the same God as the Jews, while some [the Gnostics] think there is another God).

(91) i. 19.

(92) iv. 10–11; iv. 23; v. 14.

(93) iv. 36; vi. 78.

(94) v. 41 and 50.

(95) vi. 58 ff.

(96) iv. 40; vi. 53–59.

(97) iv. 20–21.

(98) v. 52–54.

(99) iv. 6; cf. viii. 2 (they attribute their own feelings to God).

(100) v. 54, 61 ff.; vi. 53, 74; vii. 18.

(101) iv. 2 ff., 14, 18.

(102) vi. 34.

(103) iv. 33–47; v. 59 f.; vi. 49 ff.

(104) i. 17; iv. 38, 48, 50, 87. Cf. v. 65 (educated Christians say they have greater knowledge than the Jews—presumably Celsus refers to spiritual exegesis of the O.T. contrasted with Jewish literalism).

(105) vi. 66; vii. 27, 33 ff.; viii. 49.

(106) vi. 62 ff.; vii. 42, 45; viii. 21.

(107) iv. 73 ff.

(108) iv. 99.

(109) iv. 67–69 (determined cycles).

(110) iv. 62; cf. viii. 55. The doctrine of the unvarying constancy of evil, though not altogether unparalleled (cf. Alexander of Lycopolis, *adv. Manichaeos* 12) seems to have been read by Celsus out of Plato's *Theaetetus* (176) specially to counter the pressure of the Christian argument for the need of divine intervention. The myth in Plato's *Politicus* 273 DE gave decisive support to the Christian view.

(111) v. 6.

(112) v. 26, 34; vii. 68–70; viii. 1 ff., 21 ff., 55.

(113) viii. 35; viii. 1.

(114) viii. 66. According to one imperialist argument the Romans acquired universal dominion by worshipping the gods of all their

subjects so that they were rewarded for their piety (Minucius Felix, *Octavius* 6). For both pagan and Christian parallels see my note on 'Pope Damasus and the peculiar claim of Rome to St. Peter and St. Paul', *Neotestamentica et Patristica: Freundesgabe für O. Cullmann* (Leiden, 1962), pp. 313–18.

(115) i. 24; v. 41; viii. 69 (whatever name you like). Cf. the pagan correspondent of Augustine, Maximus of Madaura (Aug. *Ep.* 16), and Augustine's statement in *Ep.* 102. 10, answering Porphyry's thesis that the gods have willed to be worshipped here under one name, there under another, and that it makes no difference how the sacred rites are performed—just as languages vary while the meaning expressed is the same.

(116) vi. 42; cf. iii. 19 on the symbolism of Egyptian animal worship.

(117) i. 67; ii. 55.

(118) iv. 10; iii. 16. That Celsus's attitude to the paganism which he defends is ambivalent is well brought out by M. Simon, 'Christianisme antique et pensée païenne: rencontres et conflits', *Bulletin de la Faculté des Lettres de Strasbourg* 38 (1960), 309–23.

(119) vii. 3 and 9.

(120) viii. 60.

(121) viii. 60–63.

CHAPTER 2

(1) *Str.* i. 144 is written after the death of Commodus and therefore during the reign of the next emperor Septimius Severus.

(2) *Str.* i. 11. The absence of their names makes a significant contrast with Marcus Aurelius's catalogue of his teachers and benefactors at the beginning of his *Meditations*.

(3) *Str.* i. 101. 2 ff. transcribes much from Tatian.

(4) Eus. *H.E.* v. 10. The visit to India may be true, even though Eusebius had no documentary evidence of it, and though the story is adorned by the manifestly legendary embellishment that the Indian Christians whom Pantaenus met possessed a copy of St.

Matthew's gospel in the original Hebrew left there by St. Bartholo-
mew. In view of the trade between the Red Sea and Malabar during
the first and second centuries A.D., there is no *a priori* improbability in the story that an Egyptian Christian visited India and
found Christians there already. (See two cogent papers by A. Dihle,
'Indische Philosophen bei Clemens Alexandrinus' in *Mullus:
Festschrift für Theodor Klauser* (Münster, 1964), pp. 60–69, and
'Neues zur Thomas-Tradition' in *Jahrbuch für Antike und Christentum*
vi (1963), 54–70.)

(5) *Ecl. Proph.* 56. 2.

(6) Despite the objections of P. Nautin ('Pantène', in *Tome Com-
mémoratif du Millénaire de la bibliothèque patriarcale d'Alexandrie* (Alexandria, 1953), pp. 145–52), I do not think the opening sections of
Str. i necessarily preclude the tentative conjecture of H. I. Marrou
(*A Diognète*, Paris, 1951) that Pantaenus might be the missing
author of the anonymous letter to Diognetus (papyri attest a high
Egyptian official of this name during the last decade of the second
century). It is only for his *Stromateis* that Clement submits an
apologia; no defence is provided for the *Protreptikos* or *Paidagogos*.

(7) W. Bousset, *Jüdisch-christlicher Schulbetrieb in Alexandria und Rom*
(Göttingen, 1915), criticized by J. Munck, *Untersuchungen über
Klemens von Alexandria* (Stuttgart, 1933). Bousset's clever thesis is
less exaggerated in its treatment of Philo and Justin.

(8) W. Bauer, *Rechtgläubigkeit und Ketzerei im ältesten Christentum*
(Tübingen, 1934), pp. 49–64.

(9) See the explicit testimony of Origen (*Philocalia* 5. 7) addressing
his friend and patron Ambrose, who, 'finding an irrational and
uneducated faith intolerable, because of the lack of any better
teachers, from love to Jesus turned to doctrines which later, after
critical scrutiny, you condemned and abandoned'. Ambrose was
converted from Valentinianism to orthodoxy by Origen (Eus.
H.E. vi. 18. 1).

(10) *Str.* i. 45. 6.

(11) Celsus in Orig. *c. Cels.* i. 17, 27, 62 f.; ii. 44 (absurd justifica-
tions), 46; iii. 12, 48 ff.; iv. 42 (children's stories), 49–52, 87; v. 14
(outrageous appeal to divine omnipotence); vi. 1 ff., 14 (trapping

illiterate), 29 (allegorizers), 36 (crude anthropomorphism), 42, 45; viii. 49.

(12) *Str.* ii. 3; vi. 151.

(13) *Str.* i. 15. 4; vi. 124. 1.

(14) See H. I. Marrou's fine introduction to the *Paedagogus* prefixed to M. Harl's edition and translation of *Pd.* i, *Sources Chrétiennes* 70 (Paris, 1960).

(15) *Protr.* 57–60.

(16) *Protr.* 64 ff.

(17) Philo, *Decal.* 66; cf. *Str.* vi. 110. 3; Origen, *Comm. in Joh.* ii. 3.

(18) *Protr.* 26.

(19) *Protr.* 26, 40; *Str.* vi. 31; vii. 14.

(20) *Protr.* 39.

(21) *Protr.* 66. On Stoicism note *Str.* ii. 101. 1, rejecting the identification of God and nature.

(22) *Protr.* 68; *Str.* v. 92.

(23) *Pd.* i. 7–8; *Str.* v. 87, 94; vii. 8. 2.

(24) *Str.* v. 133. 8–9.

(25) *Protr.* 117; cf. *Str.* i. 10. 4 (scripture kindles the spark of the soul).

(26) *Protr.* 95.

(27) *Protr.* 115; cf. 99, 103, 122 (recovery from sleep). For the idea of life as leased rather than possessed freehold, cf. Lucretius iii. 971.

(28) *Protr.* 98 ff.

(29) *Str.* i. 30–32; vi. 80–90; Philo, *Congr. Erud. passim.* The idea is commonplace in second-century Platonism; cf. Albinus, *c.* vii.

(30) *Str.* i. 37.

(31) *Str.* i. 29. 1. Tutors: *Str.* i. 28. 3; cf. vi. 67, 117.

(32) *Str.* i. 57. Cf. vi. 55. 3 on eclecticism.

(33) *Str.* ii. 22 ff., 100–1; v. 95, 97; vi. 5. 1 (all later philosophers plagiarized Socrates), vi. 27. 3.

(34) *Str.* vi. 81. 4 (citing Plato's *Republic* 534 E), 156. 2, on the value

of logic. Much of *Str.* viii, consisting of notes used for questions discussed in i–vii and probably compiled after Clement's death from his papers, is devoted to logical problems. Against obscurantist Christians who think logic invented by the devil Clement retorts (*Str.* i. 44. 3–4) that this is impossible since Satan failed to detect an ingenious ambiguity in the debate with the Lord in the wilderness.

(35) *Str.* vi. 75. 3.

(36) *Str.* iv. 38. 1.

(37) At the beginning of *Str.* vii Clement warns the Christian reader that, as he is writing for pagan readers, he is not quoting the Bible as authority for his statements, but they are not to conclude from this abstinence that he is a heretic.

(38) *Str.* ii. 100–1, evidently drawn from an eclectic source.

(39) *Str.* ii. 19. 4 on the rarity of the Stoic wise man. The account of the 'true gnostic' in *Str.* vii and elsewhere incorporates many Stoic themes: see the evidence gathered by W. Völker, *Der wahre Gnostiker nach Clemens Alexandrinus* (Berlin, 1952), pp. 507 ff. For Christ as the Stoic wise man, cf. *Str.* ii. 21. Christ alone realizes the ideal of the 'true gnostic': *Str.* iv. 130. 2.

(40) *Pd.* i. 101 ff.; *Str.* ii. 19. 2. Cf. Justin, *Apol.* ii. 9. 4.

(41) The best study of Clement's debt to Stoicism is that of M. Pohlenz, 'Klemens von Alexandreia und sein hellenisches Christentum' (*Nachrichten der Akad. d. Wiss. in Göttingen*, Phil.-hist. Kl. (1943), 3).

(42) *Str.* vi. 98–99, cf. iv. 75; *Protr.* 107. 1 (the reward of finding is life with God). On the beneficent 'anger' of God, see *Pd.* i. 75–88.

(43) *Str.* vii. 67. 2. Philo anticipates Clement here (*Plant.* 90; *Immut.* 69; *Qu. Ex.* ii. 21).

(44) *Str.* iv. 14, 29, 46, 75.

(45) Justin, *Apol.* ii. 9. Cf. the objections of Celsus in Origen, *c. Cels.* iii. 78.

(46) *Pd.* i. 99.

(47) *Pd.* i. 103 distinguishes a natural morality known to all men and the commands for the good life leading to eternal life, given in the Bible. *Str.* i. 182. 1: both the natural and the revealed law

are of God. On grace cf. *Str.* v. 83. On the lack of moral power in philosophical ethics cf. *Str.* i. 80. 6.

(48) *Str.* i. 94.

(49) *Str.* i. 170. 4 denies the view of some (perhaps Valentinians?) who exalt Greek philosophy to the status of directly inspired utterance on a par with the Old Testament.

(50) *Str.* i. 50 ff. (cf. vi. 68 on the Epicureans as tares sown among the wheat of Greek philosophy).

(51) *Str.* i. 51 and 91.

(52) The plagiarism theme is recurrent; the most important passages are *Str.* i. 66 ff. and v. 86 ff., based on John x. 8 'All that came before me are thieves and robbers'. Cf. v. 100 f. (Homer and Aratus used Genesis); i. 150 and v. 30 (Pythagoras from Moses); i. 10, 165, *Pd.* ii. 18 (Plato from Moses and David), etc. For a good summary of the theme as a whole in ancient writers, Christian, Jewish, and pagan, see K. Thraede in *Reallexikon für Antike und Christentum*, s.v. 'Erfinder II'.

(53) See *Str.* i. 80; vi. 66.

(54) *Str.* vi. 57.

(55) *Str.* i. 87.

(56) *Str.* vi. 66. Cf. Origen, *c. Cels.* vii. 46, 49; *Hom. in Exod.* xi. 6.

(57) *Protr.* 70 ff.

(58) *Str.* v. 90, 102–3, 115–16.

(59) *Str.* v. 92, 93, 103, 108. The list could be much extended.

(60) *Apol.* ii. 10.

(61) *Str.* iv. 80.

(62) *Apol.* i. 46.

(63) *Str.* v. 133–4, 141.

(64) *Str.* ii. 43–44; vi. 44 ff., from Hermas, *Sim.* ix. 16, who says nothing to suggest that in Hades the Lord preached to Jews and the apostles to Gentiles.

(65) Clement's debt to Philo is large but measurable and is not to be exaggerated. He takes the thesis of *de Congressu* that philosophy

is to be the handmaid of theology (*Str.* i. 28 ff.; cf. vi. 93), the portrait of Moses from Philo's *Life* (*Str.* i. 151 ff.), much of Philo's tract on the Virtues (*Str.* ii. 78 ff., a passage so closely dependent as to be of importance for the history of the transmission of the text of Philo), the exegesis of the Mosaic tabernacle (v. 32 ff., again with much from Philo's *Life of Moses*), numerological speculations (vi. 84 ff.; 134 f.; 139 f.), the argument against anthropomorphism (v. 68), and the interpretation of God's wrath as remedial. There is, however, a marked attempt to modify many details, especially in the symbolic interpretation of scripture; e.g. the exegesis of the change of Abraham's name (*Str.* v. 8) is Christian, not a transcription of Philo, *de Mutatione Nominum*. In any event, though minor borrowings are frequent, Clement is not simply producing a hellenized Christianity precisely parallel to Philo's hellenized Judaism; his main problems (notably faith and logic, free will and determinism, and the correct evaluation of the natural order) are different from Philo's and are approached from quite another angle.

(66) *Str.* ii. 135. 3; vi. 114. 5; vii. 88. 5.

(67) *Protr.* 26. 1; 63. 1; 102.

(68) *Str.* v. 92.

(69) *Str.* v. 89. 6; 92. 3; 126. 2.

(70) *Leg. Alleg.* iii. 10; *Heres* 36; *Fuga* 46; *V. Mos.* ii. 267; cf. *Som.* ii. 45 (ordering formless *ousia*). Elsewhere Philo implies that God created matter: *Som.* i. 76, *Prov.* ap. Eus. *P.E.* vii. 21.

(71) *Leg.* 15–16.

(72) *adv. Haer.* ii. 10. 2–4; 27. 2; 28. 7; iv. 38. 3 (Massuet's sections).

(73) See J. H. Waszink's translation of and commentary on Tertullian, *adv. Hermogenem* (Ancient Christian Writers, 24; Westminster (Md.) and London, 1956).

(74) *Ecl. Proph.* 56. 2 (cf. Hippolytus, *Ref.* x. 17. 3): according to Hermogenes Christ deposited his body in the sun as suggested by Ps. xix. 4 (= xviii. 5 LXX)—perhaps an adaptation of the astrological belief that the moon presides over bodies, the sun over souls, which it receives at death; cf. Dracontius, *Rom.* x. 538 ff.

(75) *Str.* vi. 141 f.; cf. v. 141. Like Philo (*Opif.* 13, 26–28; *Leg. Alleg.* i. 2–20) Clement denies that the six days of Creation week

are intended literally (*Str.* vi. 142, 145). But he thinks Adam was created in 5592 B.C. (*Str.* i. 140–4).

(76) *Pd.* i. 88. 2.

(77) *Cod.* 109.

(78) *Pd.* i. 62. 3.

(79) *Quis dives* 33 (cf. 36).

(80) *Str.* iv. 167. 4. Clement rejects the gnostic (and Philonic) view that the coats of skins clothing Adam and Eve after their fall mean bodies (*Str.* iii. 95). Cf. p. 152, n. 56.

(81) On this affinity between Platonism and Gnosticism see *Ecl. Proph.* 17. There is a noteworthy polemic against the validity of the gnostic appeal to Plato in *Str.* iii. 12–21, but the argument is fused with the Irenaean theme that Gnosticism is an adulteration of Biblical religion with Hellenic philosophy (*adv. Haer.* ii. 14 and 21–22), so that the charge of borrowing from Greek philosophy crosses with that of misunderstanding it.

(82) *Str.* i. 94. 6; vi. 46. 3; vii. 40. 1. Cf. Tertullian, *de Anima* 53. 5–6 (similarly inconsistent).

(83) *Str.* iv. 12. 5.

(84) *Str.* iv. 164. 3.

(85) *Str.* iii. 65. 1; 100.

(86) *Str.* iii. 103. 3; cf. *Ecl. Proph.* 23.

(87) *Str.* iii. 63. 4.

(88) *Protr.* 120. Cf. *Str.* v. 88. 3 (the *pneuma* is not in us as a portion of God).

(89) *Str.* ii. 74 and 77.

(90) The nearest Clement gets is the allusive language of *Str.* vii. 10 and 12. Philo, by contrast, can write of transmigration without a qualm (*Plant.* 14; *Som.* i. 138; *Gig.* 7 ff.)—a point that has some (neglected) bearing on the interpretation of his *de Aeternitate Mundi*.

(91) *Str.* vii. 32. 8.

(92) *Str.* v. 9. 4.

(93) *Str.* vi. 156. 4.

(94) *Str.* vi. 52. Clement treats miracles as special measures within the divine providential plan of education (*Str.* vi. 28. 3). Portents like the fire on Sinai are analogous, however, to natural wonders reported in mountain caves in Persia and Britain (vi. 33). God is the cause of all, e.g. weather conditions are not caused by the sun and stars (the normal ancient view), but by God working through secondary causes (*Str.* vi. 148. 1, a view also found in Philo, *V. Mos.* i. 212, ii. 267, *Qu. Gen.* frag., ed. Marcus, ii. 217 f.).

(95) *Str.* i. 52; v. 6; vi. 12; vii. 8.

(96) *Str.* v. 7. 8.

(97) *Str.* iv. 86–87. Clement's doctrine of the Atonement is undeveloped, though he quotes Biblical language about ransom and propitiation, and calls Christ the lamb of God. Origen is the first thinker to attempt a doctrine of the Atonement which is more than biblical quotations.

(98) *Str.* vi. 132 on Peter's confession.

(99) Polemic against Docetism: *Str.* iii. 91, 102. Cf. Justin, *Dial.* 98. 1; 99. 2; 103. 8.

(100) *Pd.* i. 85. 2; *Str.* ii. 134. 2, etc.

(101) *Str.* vi. 71. 1 f.

(102) Origen, *c. Cels.* viii. 12.

(103) *Pd.* iii. 98. 1; *Str.* vii. 7. 7; cf. iv. 156 for the Son as the circle of all God's powers.

(104) *Str.* v. 6. 3. Justin liked this analogy (*Dial.* 61. 2), but Irenaeus (*adv. Haer.* ii. 13) found it dangerous because of gnostic exploitation.

(105) *Pd.* i. 4. 1; iii. 2. 1. Justin (*Dial.* 61. 1; 127. 4) strongly emphasizes the Son's ministerial role.

(106) *Pd.* i. 25.

(107) *Str.* ii. 13. 4; vii. 95; viii. 6–7; *Ecl. Proph.* 4. 2.

(108) *Str.* ii. 8. 4.

(109) *Str.* ii. 12. Note v. 6. 1 (blasphemy to demand proof of divine revelation) and v. 19 (mystery is not susceptible of vulgar demonstration). Cf. v. 85; vi. 77–78.

(110) *Pd.* i. 12 ff.; 83 f., 87.

(111) *Str.* iv. 36. 2.

(112) See esp. *Pd.* i. 25 ff. On faith as a short cut to perfection cf. *Protr.* 77. 1; 99. 4; 113. 1; *Str.* vii. 11. 2–3; 57. 3.

(113) *Str.* vi. 80, 89, 93.

(114) *Quis dives* 36. Cf. *Str.* v. 141: all men are equal before God, but differentiated by the effort with which they pursue virtue. (So also vi. 96.)

(115) *Pd.* iii. 78; *Str.* i. 35. 2 (one can be a believer without being literate, but one cannot understand the affirmations of faith without learning); vi. 165. 1 (gnosis goes beyond catechesis but abides by the Church rule).

(116) Scripture has body and soul: *Str.* vi. 132. 3. Cf. p. 150, n. 17.

(117) *Str.* vii. 35–46.

(118) *Str.* vii. 57. Probably Clement is thinking of the baptismal creed.

(119) *Str.* v. 83. 1.

(120) *Quis dives* 21; *Str.* vi. 46, vii. 10, 42.

(121) *Str.* vii. 42.

(122) *Str.* ii. 73–75.

(123) *Pd.* i. 9. 4, and many other passages. Justin anticipates this (*Ap.* i. 10. 4), but it is not a Philonic theme. On the other side, however, there is *Str.* vii. 78. 3 (the 'true gnostic' is sorry for those disciplined by punishment after death and brought to repentance 'against their will').

(124) *Pd.* i. 62 ff., 68 (righteousness), 74 (congruous with the Incarnation). Threats are medicinal: *Protr.* 8. The defence of law as an ethical principle in *Str.* i. 171 ff. is noteworthy.

(125) *Ecl. Proph.* 8. 1; 25. 4 (distinguishing destructive from saving fire in the manner of Philo, *Abr.* 157, *Heres* 136). Clement is anticipated by the Valentinians (*Exc. Theod.* 14. 4; 38. 1; 52. 2). For the development of this idea in Origen and other Christian writers see C. M. Edsman, *Le Baptême de feu* (Uppsala, 1940).

(126) *Str.* vii. 56. 3 ff.; 102. 3. Discerning fire: vii. 34. 4; cf. *Quis dives* 42 end. The term *apocatastasis* is not yet technical. Philo (*Heres* 293 f.) uses it to mean 'salvation'.

(127) *Str.* vii. 46. Cf. vi. 75, 78.

(128) *Str.* iv. 136. 5.

(129) *Str.* vii. 13, 57, 82.

(130) *Str.* ii. 6; v. 78.

(131) *Str.* v. 39–40; vi. 68.

(132) *V. Mos.* i. 158; *Leg. Alleg.* iii. 125 f.

(133) *Str.* iv. 156.

(134) *Str.* v. 71.

(135) *Pd.* i. 71. 1. Clement identifies the Son with the Monad (*Str.* iv. 156–7).

(136) *Str.* v. 78–82.

(137) 'Sober intoxication' occurs in Origen, but never in Clement. Philo's use of the oxymoron is discussed in a good monograph by H. Lewy, *Sobria Ebrietas* (Giessen, 1929).

(138) *Protr.* 120.

(139) *Str.* iii. 27; cf. ii. 117–18. A gnostic love-feast was an unrestrained affair: *Pd.* ii. 4. 3–4; *Str.* iii. 10; vii. 98.

(140) *Str.* i. 171 ff. opposes Antinomianism; cf. ii. 34; iii. 76–78; on St. Paul's harmony with the Old Testament, iv. 134.

(141) *Str.* iii. 91; cf. ii. 139. 3.

(142) *Pd.* ii. 83. 2; *Str.* iii. 66. 3.

(143) *Str.* iii. 105. But according to iv. 147–9 marriage is good, virginity better.

(144) See *Str.* iii. 82 (baptism replaces all the Old Testament lustrations for purification after intercourse).

(145) *Str.* vii. 70.

(146) *Str.* iii. 53.

(147) *Str.* ii. 88. 4 (copying Philo). Stoic moralists said the same.

(148) *Pd.* ii. 92 f.

(149) For an almost complete collection of the fragments of Musonius with English translation and introduction see C. E. Lutz in *Yale Classical Studies* x (1947). See also A. C. Geytenbeek, *Musonius Rufus and the Greek Diatribe* (Assen, 1963).

(150) *Pd.* ii. 19–34.

(151) The 'true gnostic' is allowed an occasional dinner party (*Str.* vii. 36).

(152) There are many parallels between *Quis dives* and Seneca, *de Beata vita* 20 ff. Cf. also *Pd.* ii. 120.

(153) So, for example, *Str.* iii. 96, 104; iv. 31, 147; vi. 99. 6 f.; vii. 62, 70, 75, 83.

(154) *Pd.* iii. 76–77; *Str.* vii. 36. 3. Note the protest against the cruelty of gladiatorial shows, *Str.* vii. 74. 6–7.

(155) *Pd.* iii. 57, 64 ff.

(156) *Pd.* iii. 63.

(157) *Pd.* iii. 46 ff.

(158) *Pd.* ii. 8–9; *Str.* iv. 97–98.

(159) *Str.* iv. 161. 3. Some passages, however, give moral directions for Christians in the army: *Pd.* ii. 117. 2; iii. 91. 2.

(160) *Pd.* iii. 79; *Str.* vii. 50–51.

(161) *Pd.* iii. 51–52.

(162) *Str.* vi. 90. 1.

(163) *Pd.* iii. 59. Neopythagoreans thought it wrong to wear a signet ring with a seal representing a god (see Iamblichus, *Vita Pythag.* 35. 256, and the title of Plutarch, *Qu. Conv.* iv. 9 (672 c) 'whether one may have seals representing gods or wise men').

(164) *Pd.* ii. 121. 1.

(165) *Pd.* i. 98.

(166) *Pd.* iii. 98. 1. Cf. Justin, *Apol.* ii. 2. 13 ('the school of divine virtue').

(167) *Str.* ii. 26–27, 56 ff.; iv. 145; vi. 97.

(168) *Str.* ii. 26 f.

(169) *Quis dives* 41.

(170) *Pd.* ii. 14. 3.

(171) *Str.* vi. 74, 105, 111.

(172) *Pd.* ii. 79. 2; 109. 3; *Str.* iv. 8. 7; vii. 78. 6, etc.

(173) *Str.* vii. 52; 77, etc. See on this point H. von Campenhausen, *Kirchliches Amt und geistliche Vollmacht* (Tübingen, 1953), pp. 219 f.

CHAPTER 3

(1) Quoted by Eusebius, *H.E.* vi. 19. 7.

(2) Ibid. vi. 2. 6. For a recent discussion of Eusebius's life of Origen see M. Hornschuh in *Zeitschrift f. Kirchengeschichte* 71 (1960), 1–25, who makes some valuable observations; but his radical scepticism of Eusebius suffers from the absence of any objective or rational criterion or principle.

(3) Eus. *H.E.* vi. 36. 3.

(4) Ibid. vi. 8.

(5) I have collected some of the evidence in *The Sentences of Sextus* (Cambridge, 1959), pp. 110 f. Cf. also the article 'Castration' in *Dict. d'arch. chr. et de liturgie.*

(6) *Comm. in Matt.* xv. 1 ff.

(7) *Panarion haer.* 64. 3. 11–12. Epiphanius has not, of course, a hundredth part of the authority of Eusebius as an historian; it is precisely the uncritical way in which he sets down incompatible stories that imparts value to what he says, since it argues that at least he had not the intelligence to invent the drug story, which was evidently a current slander against Origen like Epiphanius's other piece of malice that Origen's migration to Caesarea was due to shame that in the persecution at Alexandria, when offered the choice between offering incense and being abused by a homosexual Ethiopian, he had instinctively preferred the former and so became apostate and excommunicate.

Eusebius's story of the castration is sceptically regarded by K. F. Schnitzer, *Origenes über die Grundlehren der Glaubenswissenschaft* (Stuttgart, 1835), pp. xxxiii–xl (a very clear-headed discussion), and briefly by F. Böhringer, *Die Kirche Christi und ihre Zeugen* (Zürich, 1842), pp. 111 f.

(8) Eus. *H. E.* vi. 19. 6. For a recent discussion see H. Dörrie, 'Ammonios der Lehrer Plotins', in *Hermes* 83 (1955), 439–77. For a very different and (I think) highly implausible view see H. Langerbeck's paper in the *Journal of Hellenic Studies* 77 (1957), 67–74, who thinks Ammonius Saccas some sort of Christian heretic. This is at least more likely than the wild theory that Ammonius is Dionysius the Areopagite. The most sober and cautious review of the evidence is given by E. R. Dodds in *Entretiens Hardt* 5 (1960), 24 ff.

(9) For a collection of the fragments of the pagan Origen (at times adventurously interpreted) see K. O. Weber, *Origenes der Neuplatoniker* (Munich, 1962).

(10) *Comm. in Joh.* xiii. 45. 298; Jerome, *Ep.* 8. 4. 3; *Apol. adv. Rufin.* i. 18.

(11) *Quis dives* 26; *Str.* iii. 13. 1; 21. 2; iv. 2. 1; v. 140. 3; vi. 4. 2.

(12) The *de Principiis* survives as a whole only in the paraphrastic Latin translation of Rufinus, which avowedly mitigates passages likely to offend the orthodox ears of Rufinus's contemporaries, especially in books iii–iv which Rufinus treats more cautiously than i–ii. Except for substantial excerpts on the interpretation of the Bible preserved in the Greek of the *Philocalia* of Basil and Gregory Nazianzen, fragments of the original text are few, and are mainly preserved by enemies of Origen like Justinian. A selection of the most damaging passages is translated by Jerome, *Ep.* 124. So much in Rufinus's work can be paralleled, however, in the commentaries and homilies that it is possible to have reasonable confidence about the original sense except in certain instances. The standard text of Koetschau (Leipzig, 1913) is well translated into English by G. W. Butterworth (London, 1936); but the reader should be warned (*a*) that Koetschau, sceptical of Rufinus's reliability, is at times uncritically credulous towards Origen's enemies, and (*b*) that the division of books and chapters is not Origen's. See M. Harl in *Studia Patristica* (ed. F. L. Cross), iii = *T.U.* 78 (1961), pp. 57–67.

(13) Eus. *H.E.* vi. 14. 7.

(14) *Comm. in Joh.* x. 5. 20.

(15) Ibid. i. 4. 23.

(16) *Comm. in Matt.* xv. 3.

(17) *de Princ.* iv. 2. 4; *Hom. in Lev.* v. 1 and 5; *Hom. in Num.* ix. 7. Cf. Philo, *V. Cont.* 78; Clement, *Str.* vi. 132. 3. On Origen's principles of Biblical exegesis the best study is that of H. de Lubac, *Histoire et Esprit* (Paris, 1950); his *Exégèse médiévale* I. i (Paris, 1959), pp. 198 ff., gives a masterly account of Origen's influence on later commentaries. On typology see especially J. Daniélou, *Sacramentum Futuri* (Paris, 1949); R. P. C. Hanson, *Allegory and Event* (London, 1959); R. M. Grant, *The Letter and the Spirit* (London, 1957).

(18) *de Princ.* iv. 2. 1.

(19) *in Matt. Ser.* 61.

(20) See the exposition of Matt. xiii. 36 in *Comm. in Matt.* x. 1, *c. Cels.* iii. 21, and *Dial. c. Heracl.*, 1st ed. p. 152 Scherer (the pagination of the first edition is given in the margin of the second).

(21) *c. Cels.* ii. 66; *Comm. in Joh.* i. 7. 43, etc.

(22) *Comm. in Joh.* i. 9 ff. The embryo of Origen's idea is found in Justin's contrast (*Ap.* ii. 6) between the nameless Father and the many names of Christ (cf. *Dial.* 34. 2). That conceptions of God vary according to the believer's capacity is in Philo, *Mut.* 19 ff.

(23) *Comm. in Joh.* xix. 6. 38; cf. Philo, *Leg. Alleg.* iii. 125 f.

(24) *c. Cels.* ii. 64; iv. 16; vi. 68, etc.

(25) *in Matt. Ser.* 50, 56, esp. 70; *Comm. in Matt.* xii. 30, 32. There is a direct attack on materialistic notions of heaven in *de Princ.* ii. 11. 2.

(26) *de Princ.* ii. 10. 5. Philo interprets Hades as tortures of conscience (*Congr.* 57).

(27) *c. Cels.* iii. 78–79; iv. 10, 19; vi. 26, 72.

(28) Ibid. v. 15 ff. (Note esp. 22, 'Let no one think I am one of those who deny the Church's doctrine of resurrection; I preserve both the doctrine of the Church and the greatness of God's promise.') Especially important for Origen's position is the fragment on Psalm i preserved by Methodius, *de Resurr.* i. 20 ff. and by

Epiphanius, *Panarion haer.* 64. 12; the other main texts are *de Princ.* ii. 10–11; iii. 6. 5–9; *Comm. in Matt.* xvii. 29–33. No text of Origen in either Greek original or translation contains the doctrine ascribed to him in the sixth century that resurrection bodies are spherical (the sphere being the perfect shape according to *Timaeus* 33 B, cf. 44 D, and also the shape of the cosmic god of the Stoics; cf. Seneca, *Apocolocyntosis* 8 of Claudius's rotundity resembling a Stoic god, and Ovid, *Fasti* vi. 271–2). But he believed that the stars have souls (since capable of sin, Job xxv. 5, cf. *Comm. in Joh.* i. 35. 257; *Comm. in Rom.* iii. 6) and spherical bodies (*de Orat.* 31. 3). Plotinus says that souls in heaven, despite their astral spherical bodies, recognize one another by inner character (iv. 4(28). 5. 18; cf. iii. 4(15). 6. 18 ff.). The Platonic and the Christian are fused in Dante's *Paradiso* xiv where the holy souls awaiting resurrection are starry spheres.

For discussion see my remarks in *Harv. Theol. Rev.* 41 (1948), pp. 83–102; A.-J. Festugière in *Revue des sciences philos. et théol.* 43 (1959), 81–86.

(29) Origen's attacks on chiliasm, though rare, are decisive: *Comm. in Matt.* xvii. 35; *de Orat.* xxvii. 13; *Comm. in Cant. Cantic.* prol., (p. 66 Baehrens); frag. in Methodius, *de creatis* 12 (p. 499 Bonwetsch); Origen, *Hom. in Ps. XXXVI*, 3. 10 (XII. 196 f. Lommatzsch).

(30) *de Orat.* 31. 3; *Comm. in Rom.* ix. 41.

(31) Irenaeus, *adv. Haer.* ii. 28. 2–3.

(32) *c. Cels.* vii. 42 ff., well interpreted by Festugière, *La Révélation d'Hermès Trismégiste* iv. 119–123.

(33) *Comm. in Joh.* xiii. 25. Note ii. 23. 149 f.: Because both Father and Son are light, some mistakenly think the *ousia* of the Son not distinct from the Father's (i.e. the argument Justin tries to meet in *Dial.* 128).

(34) Philo, *Heres* 240; *Gig.* 12; *Som.* i. 138 f.; *Opif.* 168; *Post. C.* 145; *Qu. Gen.* iv. 87; *Qu. Ex.* ii. 40.

(35) *de Princ.* ii. 8. 3. Cf. Philo, *Som.* i. 31. See Waszink's commentary on Tert. *de Anima* 25. 2.

(36) e.g. *Comm. in Joh.* xxxii. 18. 218; *Hom. in Luc.* 36. Cf. ch. 4, n. 74. Again the idea is Philonic, e.g. *Leg. Alleg.* iii. 84.

(37) *de Princ.* ii. 1. 1 f. The Platonist Albinus (in Stobaeus i. 49. 37) anticipates Origen's view, saying that souls descend by a mistaken choice, not by a natural destiny resulting from emanations. There is a polemic against this view in Hierocles, *Comm. in Carmen Aureum* i. 1, xi. 17–20 (Mullach, pp. 420 a, 443 a).

(38) *de Princ.* ii. 1. 4. See also *Comm. in Gen.* ap. Eus. *P.E.* vii. 20.

(39) *c. Cels.* iv. 54 ff.

(40) *Opif.* 75; *Conf.* 179; *Abr.* 143; *Fuga* 68 ff.

(41) *c. Cels.* iv. 66; vi. 53.

(42) *de Princ.* ii. 2–3; iii. 6. Both Rufinus and Jerome tendentiously confuse the text. See Karl Müller in *Sitzungsber. Berl. Akad.* 1919, pp. 622 ff.

(43) Cf., however, *de Orat.* 26. 6, where the first view appears.

(44) Cf. *Frag. in Joh.* 13 (p. 495 Preuschen).

(45) *c. Cels.* iii. 41; iv. 57; vi. 77.

(46) *de Princ.* i. 7. 5; iii. 5. 4; *Comm. in Rom.* vii. 4; *Hom. in Num.* xxviii. 2.

(47) *c. Cels.* vii. 50.

(48) The argument is a commonplace of the Stoic theodicy, of which Origen made full use.

(49) *de Princ.* iii. 2. 1–2; *Hom. in Gen.* ii. 6.

(50) *Hom. in Lev.* iv. 6. For a striking anticipation see Philo, *V. Mos.* ii. 68 (Moses practised continence so as to be ready at any time to be the medium of inspired prophecy). Likewise *de Spec. Leg.* i. 150.

(51) *Hom. in Gen.* iii. 6; *Comm. in Matt.* xiv. 1–2.

(52) *Hom. in Lev.* viii. 3; cf. *c. Cels.* vii. 50; *Comm. in Rom.* v. 9; *Hom. in Luc.* 14.

(53) *Comm. in Rom.* v. 1 and 4.

(54) *Hom. in Lev.* viii. 3. Origen takes the idea from Philo, *Ebr.* 208.

(55) *Comm. in Matt.* x. 12; xii. 4.

(56) See *c. Cels.* iv. 40; *Sel. in Gen.* (VIII. 58 Lommatzsch). Clement had rejected this interpretation (*Str.* iii. 95). Ambrose (*ep.* 49. 4) accepts it. It appears also in Porphyry (*de Abst.* i. 31).

(57) *Comm. in Joh.* xxxii. 2; *Comm. in Matt.* x. 24; *Hom. in Luc.* 35. The truth that petty dishonesties and drunkennesses are sins before God no less than pride and other vices is providentially not understood by ignorant believers who, not having the capacity to understand that divine punishment for sin is remedial, would lose heart if they knew: *Hom. in Lev.* xiv. 3; *Hom. in Jerem.* xx. 3; *Dial. c. Heracl.* 1st ed., p. 142 Scherer.

(58) *de Princ.* ii. 6. 6.

(59) *c. Cels.* iii. 41.

(60) *Comm. in Rom.* i. 6; *de Princ.* ii. 6. 2.

(61) *Dial. c. Heracl.*, 1st ed., p. 136; *Comm. in Joh.* xx. 11. 86; xxxii. 18. 218 ff. Origen's argument entirely anticipates the standard Cappadocian objection to Apollinarianism as formulated especially by Gregory Nazianzen; cf. Athanasius, *Tomus ad Antiochenos* 7. Origen attacks those who think the Logos assumed a body, not a human soul, in *de Princ.* iv. 4. 4.

(62) *de Princ.* ii. 8. 5; *Hom. in Lev.* xii. 5.

(63) *Comm. in Cant. Cantic.* ii (p. 153 Baehrens).

(64) *c. Cels.* iii. 14; iv. 32; *Hom. in Iesu Nave* vii. 7.

(65) *de Orat.* xv–xvi; *c. Cels.* v. 4–5; viii. 26.

(66) *c. Cels.* v. 39; vi. 61; vii. 57. Cf. *de Orat.* xv. 1; *Comm. in Joh.* ii. 2; x. 37.

(67) *c. Cels.* viii. 12; *Comm. in Matt.* xvii. 14; *Comm. in Joh.* ii. 10; x. 37.

(68) *de Orat.* xv. 1. See also note 33 above.

(69) *c. Cels.* iii. 28.

(70) *Comm. in Joh.* ii. 8.

(71) For the analogy of the Bible and the Incarnation see *in Matt. Ser.* 27; *Hom. in Exod.* xii. 4; *Hom. in Lev.* i. 1. Cf. ch. 4, n. 13.

(72) *Comm. in Rom.* i. 4; *de Princ.* ii. 8. 7; iii. 6. 8; iv. 2. 4, etc. Jerome (*Ep.* 124. 12), takes exception to Origen's opinion which is paralleled in Irenaeus (*adv. Haer.* iv. 9. 2) and Methodius (*Symp.* ix. 2).

(73) *de Orat.* 5; cf. *Frag. in 1 Cor.* iii. 21 f., ed. Jenkins in *JTS* ix. 353.

(74) *Comm. in Rom.* ix. 1.

(75) *de Orat.* xxviii. 9 f. Origen's doctrine of penitence is extremely complex (and controversial); it is bound up with his ambivalent attitude to the clergy in general, on the one hand profoundly respectful of the office, on the other hand sternly critical of clerical conduct in practice. In Origen's thought about the Church a high sacramentalism crosses with an anti-clerical pietistic strain, and the resulting inconsistencies have led to very diverse interpretations of his words. The most dispassionate account is that of H. von Campenhausen, *Kirchliches Amt und Geistliche Vollmacht* pp. 287 ff.

(76) *Hom. in Num.* xxv. 6.

(77) Origen is the first to read into 1 Cor. iii. 10–15 the doctrine of an ultimate purification for all. For a good examination of the history of this exegesis see J. Gnilka, *Ist I Kor. 3, 10–15 ein Schrift-zeugnis für das Fegfeuer?* (Düsseldorf, 1955).

(78) *Comm. in Joh.* vi. 58. 297; *Hom. in Lev.* viii. 5.

(79) *c. Cels.* iv. 65; *Comm. in Joh.* ii. 13. 97.

(80) *Comm. in Joh.* xx. 28. 254.

(81) *Hom. in Num.* xx. 3; *Hom. in Lev.* vii. 2; *Comm. in Joh.* xix. 14 and 21, etc.

(82) *de Orat.* xxvii. 15 and many passages.

(83) *de Princ.* i. 3. 8; *Comm. in Joh.* x. 42.

(84) *Comm. in Matt.* xii. 34; *Comm. in Cant. Cantic.* i. (p. 103 Baehrens): once the soul attains to union with the very *ousia* of the Logos, it is bound by the chains of love and can never again remove, being one spirit with him. *Comm. in Rom.*, Tura papyrus frag. (p. 208 Scherer) distinguishes the indefectibility of faith, which is certain, from that of righteousness which can be lost. (Cf. *JTS* N.S. x (1959), 36).

CHAPTER 4

(1) Vaticanus gr. 1742, fol. 1ʳ, printed (from Milanese copies of this MS.) by Koetschau, *Die Textüberlieferung der Bücher des Origenes gegen Celsus* (*T.U.* 6, 1, 1889), pp. 73–74, corrected by G. Mercati in *Bessarione* 24 (1920), 133. My translation is an abbreviating

paraphrase. The quotations are, respectively, from Cassiodorus, *Inst.* i. 1. 8 (p. 14 Mynors); Gregory Nazianzen as quoted in Suidas, s.v. 'Origenes' (i. 619 Adler), but the words are not, so far as I know, to be found among his writings; and Justinian (paraphrased), *Edictum adv. Origenem*, Migne, *P.G.* 86. 949 B = E. Schwartz, *A.C.O.* III. 190–1. Origen is made responsible for Arianism by Epiphanius, *Panarion haer.* 64. 4. 2–4. Marcellus of Ancyra seems to have anticipated his view; see below, p. 159, n. 21.

(2) On Evagrius and the Origenist controversy of the sixth century see the masterly study by A. Guillaumont, *Les Kephalaia Gnostica d'Evagre le Pontique* (Paris, 1962). The primary source for the history of the Origenist monks in Palestine, Cyril of Scythopolis, can now be read in A.-J. Festugière's well-annotated French translation (*Les Moines d'Orient* iii, Paris, 1962–3).

(3) It is now agreed that, although the Acts of the Fifth General Council (most fully preserved in a Latin translation) do not include a process of condemnation against Origen, nevertheless the Council did in fact condemn him by receiving a formal letter on the subject addressed to it by Justinian (preserved by Georgius Hamartolus, *Chron.* iv. 218, *P.G.* 110. 780–92). The fact of the Council's action, attested by Cyril of Scythopolis (*Vita S. Sabae* 90, *T.U.* 49, 2, p. 199 Schwartz) and by Evagrius (*H.E.* iv. 38), was commonly denied before the monograph of F. Diekamp, *Die origenistischen Streitigkeiten* (Münster, 1899).

(4) See an interesting paper by E. Wind, 'The Revival of Origen', in *Studies in Art and Literature for Belle da Costa Greene*, ed. D. Miner (Princeton, 1954), pp. 412–24. Pico's *Conclusiones Nongentae* (1486) was placed on the Index, *inter alia*, for defending Origen.

(5) F. L. Cross, *Darwell Stone* (Westminster, 1943), p. 204.

(6) *Hom. in Luc.* 25 (p. 151 Rauer[2]).

(7) '. . . Origenem quem post apostolos ecclesiarum magistrum nemo nisi imperitus negabit': Jerome's preface to the *Onomasticon* or *Liber de nominibus hebraicis* (Vallarsi[2], III. 3). Similar praise occurs in the famous preface to Jerome's translation of Origen's homilies on the Song of Songs: 'In other books Origen surpassed everyone else, but in the Song of Songs he surpassed himself'

(p. 26, Baehrens), and in the long catalogue of Origen's works in Jerome, *Ep.* 33. A classified list of Jerome's references to Origen, showing how his mind changed as the controversy mounted and his own reputation was endangered, is given by F. Cavallera, *S. Jérôme, sa vie et son œuvre* ii (Louvain, 1922), pp. 115–27.

(8) Gregory Thaumaturgus, *Paneg.* 15: As exegete Origen is inspired by the Author of the inspired scripture.

(9) Pamphilus speaks in sorrow and anger of critics who, ignoring Origen's personal humility and expressed desire for correction and pardon, complained that his admirers put him on a par with the apostles and prophets (XXIV. 297, Lommatzsch). This charge is levelled in just these words by Marcellus of Ancyra (see Eusebius, *c. Marc.* i. 4, p. 21, Klostermann) who, paradoxically, appears to have drawn the material for his attack in part from Pamphilus's work, since he immediately quotes a passage from *de Princ.* iv. 4. 1 which coincides in beginning and ending with a quotation made in Pamphilus's apology. The extent to which Origen's admirers resented the criticisms may be fairly conjectured from the censure which the Council of Antioch of 268 passed upon Paul of Samosata for his irreverence in speaking of dead exegetes (Eus. *H.E.* vii. 30. 9).

(10) *Hom. in Lev.* i. 1; vii. 4–5; xiii. 3. For defence against arbitrariness cf. *Hom. in Exod.* xiii. 2; *Hom. in Ezech.* ii. 5.

(11) *Comm. in Joh.* x. 18. 110. See also the reply to Celsus's view that the Bible is incapable of being interpreted allegorically without violence to the text, and that allegory is merely a sophisticated device for avoiding embarrassment (*c. Cels.* iv. 48–51). Celsus himself finds an allegory of the cosmic conflict between good and evil in Homer, Pherecydes, and Athena's battle with the Giants represented on the ceremonial robe at the annual festival of the Panathenaea (vi. 42), an interpretation frequent in the sixth-century Platonist Proclus (*in Tim.* I. 85, 134, 167, Diehl). Celsus, Porphyry, and the Platonist critics of Christianity had no objection in principle to allegorical interpretation as such. They too had their sacred texts to reconcile and to expound for modern use, and allegory was indispensable to them.

(12) *Hom. in Jerem.* xx. 8.

(13) Origen does not find it difficult to justify allegory and spiritual interpretation. If it is accepted that the Bible is a collection of in-spired writings intended by the divine author to instruct each generation in timeless truth, it cannot be what in part it appears to be, viz. ancient history or geography or ceremonial legislation for a bygone age. Only spiritual interpretation gives these parts of the Bible a contemporary, existential relevance. Against objectors Origen can appeal to the authority of St. Paul (1 Cor. ix. 9, etc.). In detail his 'objective' principles or rules are the same as Philo's: one finds the clues to the hidden meaning by studying the sym-bolism of numbers, or the interpretation of Hebrew proper names of persons and places, or by attending to grammatical oddities in the text. Anything that is literally impossible or morally offensive may confidently be accepted as a providentially given clue to the necessity of spiritual exegesis. The danger of dissolving all history, apparent in the gnostic allegories of the Valentinians, induced caution, at least in regard to the New Testament (*Comm. in Joh.* xx. 20). But Origen believes it possible to avoid private, unrestricted fantasy (*a*) by taking scripture, not piecemeal, but as a whole (*Comm. in Joh.* x. 18. 107; *in Matt. Ser.* 47; *Hom. in Num.* xii. 2; *Hom. in Ps. XXXVI*, 3. 6), (*b*) by interpreting the obscure passages on the basis of the plain, comparing text with text (*c. Cels.* vii. 11; *in I Cor.* ii. 14, ed. Jenkins, *JTS* ix. 240), (*c*) by checking with the teaching of other expositors (*Hom. in Lev.* xvi. 5; *Hom. in Num.* xxvi. 6)—for whom Origen has so great a respect that he is con-tinually referring to the expositions of orthodox predecessors, and his exegetical writings are therefore a mine of information about anonymous Christian explanation of scripture before his time. See on this Harnack, *Der kirchengeschichtliche Ertrag der exegetischen Arbeiten des Origenes* ii (*T.U.* 42, 4, 1919), pp. 4–33. Origen often insists that the central key to the interpretation of the Bible is Christ himself, who is the principle of unity in scripture (e.g. *Comm. in Joh.* v. 6; *Comm. in Matt.* xv. 32; xvii. 12) and is so closely bound up with it that the relation of human and divine elements in scrip-ture is analogous to that in the incarnate Lord (*in Matt. Ser.* 27; *Hom. in Exod.* xii. 4; *Hom. in Lev.* i. 1; cf. Clement, *Str.* vi. 126. 3; 132. 4).

(14) Eus. *H.E.* vi. 8. 4; 23. 4; Jerome, *de Vir. inl.* 54; Pamphilus in Photius, *Bibl.* 118.

(15) According to *de Princ.* i. 6. 3 the question whether the spirits who are now devils will one day be converted, or whether long wickedness has passed from habit to being virtually nature, is left to the judgement of the reader, who is, however, bidden to remember that the latter view implies an eternal cosmic dualism. The destruction of 'the last enemy' means not the destruction of any created being or substance, but the transformation of the hostile will by the omnipotent God to whom nothing is impossible or incurable—though the process of conversion may take time (iii. 6. 5). The principle so stated is no mere speculation of the young Origen. It is formally and repeatedly stated in the *contra Celsum*, one of his last works; especially viii. 72 (none is so evil as to be beyond the healing power of the Logos) and iii. 69: 'Every rational soul possesses the same nature, and the Creator has made no nature wicked. But many have become evil by upbringing, perversion, and environment, so that in some evil has become second nature. . . . For the divine Logos to change evil which has become second nature is not only not impossible but is not even very difficult, if only a man admits that he must trust himself to the supreme God. . . . If for some it is very hard to change, the cause lies in their will. . . . To say it is impossible is to find fault with the Creator of the rational being rather than with the creature.' The doctrine depends in part on Origen's axiom that all rational creatures possess a single *ousia* or nature. That this axiom did not come under suspicion of heresy until a late stage in the Origenist controversy is evident from Athanasius, *Or. c. Arianos*, ii. 41, who takes its truth for granted.

(16) The text of the disputation between Origen and Candidus was still circulating in the time of Jerome (*Ep.* 33. 4. 4; *Apol. adv. Rufin.* ii. 19). Origen complained that the version published by Candidus was not accurate. For analogies cf. Basil, *Ep.* 210. 5 (garbled minutes of a dispute between Gregory Thaumaturgus and Aelian); Possidius, *Vita S. Aug.* 17 (Augustine unwilling to dispute without a precise record being taken, for fear of garbled accounts).

(17) The sources for this story are Rufinus, *de Adulteratione librorum Origenis* (*P.G.* 17. 624–6; now available in a fine critical edition by M. Simonetti in *Corpus Christianorum*, series latina 20, 1961), and the critical comments thereon by Jerome, *Apol. adv. Rufin.* ii. 18–19. A whitewashing account of Demetrius's censure of Origen

appeared in Pamphilus's *Apology* (in Photius, *Bibl.* 118; cf. Eus. *H.E.* vi. 8. 4–5; Jerome, *Ep.* 33. 5), according to which there was no questioning of Origen's doctrine, but only a dispute about technical matters of Church order and canon law, while the motives of Demetrius are made out to be no more than personal envy. For a critical review of the evidence see the important paper by C. C. Richardson, 'The Condemnation of Origen', in *Church History* 6 (1937), 50–64. That the prime issue concerned his doctrine is clear from the fact that in the subsequent controversy Origen had to defend himself from the charge of heresy (Eus. *H.E.* vi. 36. 4). Long before, Origen had had occasion to express fear that inattentive readers might suspect his work On First Principles of being heretical (*de Princ.* i. 6. 1).

(18) *Comm. in Joh.* vi. 1 ff. (an apologia for delay in resuming the work begun at Alexandria).

(19) Jerome, *Ep.* 84. 10 (to Pammachius and Oceanus, written in 399): 'Origen himself in the letter that he wrote to Fabian bishop of Rome expresses regret for having put certain things in writing, and ascribes the responsibility for this rashness to Ambrose who had published openly writings intended for a private circle.' Eusebius (*H.E.* vi. 36. 4) says that this letter, like others which Origen wrote to bishops at this time, 'concerned his orthodoxy'. But it is evident from Jerome's wording that Origen withdrew nothing; he only regretted having deep truths broadcast before a promiscuous audience, like Demetrius, unworthy to receive them.

(20) *Comm. in Joh.* vi. 46. 241 comments on the way of some who adopt a negative attitude before they have learnt what the question under discussion actually is.

(21) Epiphanius, *Panarion haer.* 64. 72. 9. As early as about 327 Marcellus of Ancyra tries to undermine the authority of Origen's theology of the Trinity by saying that he began to teach and preach too soon after he had been studying philosophy and was led astray by the Platonism with which his mind was filled (Eusebius, *contra Marcellum* i. 4). For Epiphanius's attitude to Origen see the excellent article on Epiphanius by W. Schneemelcher in *Reallexikon für Antike und Christentum* (1961).

(22) See Clement, *Pd.* ii. 77–82, where the New Testament

exhortations to watch with loins girded are interpreted as part of a discussion of discipline in regard to sleep.

(23) *Ep.* I. ii. 1–4, naming the Stoic Chrysippus and the Platonist Crantor. It is only fair to add that this remark must be seen in the perspective of the ancient debate whether truth is learnt from the poets or from the philosophers, discussed at least since Plato's exclusion of Homer from his ideal educational system. Plutarch's tract 'How a young man should understand poems' (*Mor.* 14–37) gives a long examination of hermeneutic rules for demythologizing the poets, and thinks that the shock of the transition from poetry to philosophy will be mitigated if the young are educated on poetic excerpts selected to show the essential harmony of poets and philosophers. (For this theme cf. Seneca, *Ep.* 9. 20–21.) But Galen (*de Placitis Hippocratis et Platonis* ii. 213 ff., iii. 300 ff.) sharply criticizes the Stoic Chrysippus for filling his philosophical writings with poetic citations. The sophists' habit of quoting tags from Euripides to justify doubtful morality is caricatured in the *Frogs* of Aristophanes (1471). Socrates was accused of doing the same (Xenophon, *Mem.* i. 2. 56–59). Anthologies of excerpts from the poets and philosophers were widely used in education, and many of Clement's collections are transcribed from these sources. For a fuller discussion see my article, 'Florilegium', in *Reallexikon für Antike und Christentum*, forthcoming.

(24) Whether Origen took this name himself, as Epiphanius censoriously says (*Panarion haer.* 64. 72. 1), or whether the name was given him by others, as Jerome thinks, cannot be decided on the thin evidence (Eus. *H.E.* vi. 14. 10; Jerome, *de Vir. inl.* 54; *Ep.* 33. 4. 11; Photius, *Bibl.* 118). But probably Jerome is right; it is more charitable to think so.

(25) That the allusion in *c. Cels.* i. 31 to *Iliad* v. 1–3 is a commonplace is clear from Clement, *Str.* i. 161. 3. The same may hold good for others, as *c. Cels.* ii. 61, etc.

(26) Eus. *H.E.* vi. 19. On this indissoluble unity in late antiquity see Glanville Downey, 'Julian and Justinian and the unity of faith and culture', in *Church History* 28 (1959).

(27) *Comm. in Joh.* i. 34. 246; cf. i. 37. 269.

(28) *de Princ.* i. 3. 1 f.

(29) Christ is the true and perfect image of God; man is made 'after the image' which is the Logos (*Comm. in Joh.* i. 17. 104–5; ii. 3. 20; *c. Cels.* vi. 63; vii. 66; *Hom. in Gen.* i. 13; *Hom. in Luc.* 8, p. 48 Rauer², etc.).

(30) *Exh. Mart.* 47; *de Princ.* ii. 11. 4; *Sel. in Ps.* (XI. 424, Lommatzsch); *Comm. in Cant. Cantic.* i (p. 91 Baehrens).

(31) *Hom. in Gen.* xiii. 4; *Hom. in Num.* xxiv. 2; *Hom. in Ezech.* xiii. 2.

(32) *c. Cels.* iii. 40. The only late Platonist opponent of Christianity who seriously comes near to conceding this point is Porphyry in his letter to 'Anebo' (well edited with indispensable commentary by A. R. Sodano, Naples, 1958).

(33) *c. Cels.* i. 4; ii. 5.

(34) *Hom. in Luc.* 35 (p. 196 Rauer²).

(35) *Comm. in Rom.* iii. 7; viii. 2; ix. 24.

(36) *Hom. in Luc.* 8 (pp. 50–51 Rauer²).

(37) Tura papyrus fragment of the commentary on Romans, ed. Scherer, 166, 1 ff., qualified by 'I think'. Cf. the discussion in *c. Cels.* iii. 69: Celsus says that 'the sinless have a better life in heaven'; Origen replies that in fact none are sinless, though a very few may remain without sin after conversion and only so with the grace of the divine Word. Christ alone is sinless and perfect, cf. i. 70; *Comm. in Joh.* xxxii. 7.

(38) *de Princ.* iii. 1. 17 for the possibility of repentance hereafter; *c. Cels.* iii. 81, 'The blessed future life will be for those alone who have accepted the religion of Jesus and who reverence the Creator of the universe with a pure and untainted worship.'

(39) Origen's most sympathetic statement of the Greek moral ideal occurs in his *Homilies on Jeremiah* (vi. 3). But elsewhere he comments that it is an ideal of human dignity rather than of the service and love of God: cf. *Hom. in Num.* i. 2, 'Est enim virtus animi quam Graeci philosophi docent. sed haec non pertinet ad numerum dei; non enim pro deo sed pro gloria exercetur humana.' Similarly xi. 7.

Origen is characteristically reserved towards what is fastidious and sophisticated, as ideals on which he has turned his back. Cf. the defence of Christian popular style in *c. Cels.* vi. 1 ff., and the profound observation in one of his Homilies on the 36th Psalm (v. 6): 'No virtue is more highly prized in scripture than innocence; it is a measure of the world's corruption that it is commonly taken for stupidity.'

(40) *Comm. in Joh.* ii. 16. 112.

(41) *de Princ.* ii. 3. 4; *c. Cels.* iv. 67–68; v. 20.

(42) *c. Cels.* vi. 71.

(43) See *c. Cels.* iv. 74–99. For the philosopher's responsibility for the moral consequences of his opinions cf. iv. 83, and similar views in Epictetus ii. 20. 34.

(44) On Philo see P. Barth, 'Die stoische Theodizee bei Philon', *Philos. Abhandlungen für M. Heinze* (Berlin, 1906).

(45) *Hom. in Ezech.* x. 1; *Hom. in Lev.* xiv. 3.

(46) *de Princ.* i. 8. 4: 'wavering and weak'; *c. Cels.* vii. 33: 'our will is too weak to achieve purity of heart without grace'; *Hom. in Ps. XXXVI*, 4. 1; *Hom. in Luc.* 11 (p. 68); 31 (p. 178 Rauer²). A good will is God's gift: *Comm. in Matt.* x. 6.

(47) *de Princ.* ii. 3. 4.

(48) Cf. Gregory of Nyssa's remark that Aetius went beyond Arius in applying the syllogisms of Aristotelian logic (*c. Eunomium* i. 46).

(49) The essential material is collected by G. Bardy, 'Origène et l'Aristotélisme', *Mélanges Glotz* (Paris, 1932), i. 75 ff.; A.-J. Festugière, *L'Idéal religieux des grecs et l'Évangile* (Paris, 1932), pp. 253–4; H. Crouzel, *Origène et la philosophie* (Paris, 1962), pp. 29–34. For the view that indirect Aristotelian influence can be seen, cf. Hal Koch, *Pronoia und Paideusis* (Berlin, 1932), p. 205.

(50) It was an old thesis of the eclectic philosophers that Aristotle was a good Platonist: see Cicero's *Academica* I. 4. 17 where Varro explains that Plato established a philosophy which, under the two names of Academic and Peripatetic, was really one and the same system. The late neoplatonist commentators on Aristotle, such as Syrianus, regard Aristotle as an invaluable preparation for the study of Plato who represents the higher mysteries (Marinus, *Vita Procli* 13). Cf. Damascius, *Vita Isidori* = Photius, *Bibl.* 242 (337 b, 9 ff.).

(51) Eus. *P.E.* xv. 4–9. Eusebius quotes Atticus to prove that where Aristotle and Plato disagree, Plato and the Bible agree.

(52) Hierocles in Photius, *Bibl.* 251 (461 a, 31).

(53) See the commentary on Psalm iv in *Philocalia* 26.

(54) *c. Cels.* i. 10; similarly Gregory Nazianzen, *Or.* 27 (*Theol.* 1). 10.

(55) *Hom. in Jerem.* xx. 1. Albinus, (*Didaskalikos* 6, p. 159, 35, Hermann) explains that the ten categories formed part of the teaching of Plato and may be found in the *Parmenides*.

(56) For example the Aristotelian definitions of *telos* (*Sel. in Ps.*, XI. 351 Lommatzsch) in a fragment, conjecturally but with fair probability ascribed to Origen, prefixed to a catena on the Psalms in codex Paris. gr. 146, cod. Laurentianus VI, 3, etc. This fragment is briefly discussed by Klostermann in *N.T. Studien für G. Heinrici* (Leipzig, 1914), p. 249.

(57) For the Stoic doctrine of cosmic sympathy see a succinct account in Sextus Empiricus, *adv. Math.* ix (= *adv. Phys.* i), 75–85. For Stoic opposition to the Aristotelian 'fifth essence', cf. *c. Cels.* iv. 56, and Porphyry's *Symmikta Zetemeta* iv, quoted in a *scholion* on Basil's *Hexaemeron* in a ninth-century manuscript at Genoa, printed by G. Pasquali in *Nachrichten der Akademie d. Wiss. zu Göttingen*, 1910, frag. XXX, p. 201 οἴονται γὰρ οἱ Ζηνώνειοι τούτου [*sc.* πέμπτου σώματος] παραδεχθέντος ἀναιρεῖσθαι τῶν ἐν γῇ τὴν πρὸς τὰ κατ' οὐρανὸν συμπάθειαν. In his commentary on the *Timaeus* Porphyry rejected the Aristotelian doctrine (frag. 60 Sodano = Philoponus, *de Aet. Mundi* xiii. 15, p. 522 Rabe).

(58) Critolaus according to Macrobius, *in Somn. Scip.* i. 14. 20; Tertullian, *de Anima* 5; cf. Iamblichus in Stobaeus i. 49. 32, pp. 366–7 Wachsmuth (a passage translated and richly annotated by Festugière, *La Révélation d'Hermès Trismégiste* iii. 188).

(59) Cf. Philo, *Heres* 283, for some who say the saint's soul at death returns to the ether as being of a fifth essence, while his body returns to the four elements here below.

(60) *c. Cels.* iii. 72.

(61) *de Princ.* iv. 3. 4.

(62) See the catena fragment on 1 Cor. iv. 6, ed. Jenkins, *JTS* ix. 357. Origen's comments on the same text in the commentary on St. John (xiii. 5–6) show much more interest in its implication that there are truths of religion that transcend the possibility of being written. The analogy of the Incarnation is never far from Origen's mind in this context. Cf. *Comm. in Joh.* ii. 8. 61: even at the very summit of the soul's mystical contemplation there is no forgetting the Incarnation. On the other hand, Church festivals are provided as a concession to weaker brethren (*c. Cels.* viii. 22–23).

(63) *de Princ.* ii. 8. 7; iv. 3. 12–13, cf. iii. 6. 8; *Comm. in Rom.* i. 4.

(64) *de Orat.* 5. Cf. ch. 3, n. 72.

(65) For an account of Origen's doctrine of the Church and hierarchy see H. von Campenhausen, *Kirchliches Amt und geistliche Vollmacht*, pp. 262–91.

(66) Among many passages see especially *Comm. in Joh.* ii. 24. 156–7; 28. 171 ff. (the ascent to the darkness where God dwells, cf. *c. Cels.* vi. 17); *c. Cels.* vii. 38; *de Orat.* 9. 2.

(67) *de Princ.* i. 1. 7; *c. Cels.* vi. 63. Theodoret (*Qu. Gen.* i, *P.G.* 80. 113) preserves a fragment of Origen attacking Melito's opinion that God is corporeal like man, his image.

(68) *in Matt. Ser.* 38; *Comm. in Rom.* v. 8 (VII. 47 Lommatzsch); Clement, *Exc. Theod.* 28.

(69) Jerome, *Ep.* 124. 4 (*ad Avitum*); cf. the excerpt from Justinian's *contra Origenem* (Schwartz, *A.C.O.* III. 211, excerpt xv) printed by Koetschau in *de Princ.* i. 8. 4. The discussion in the original text of *de Principiis* was probably less negative and peremptory than Rufinus would have us believe; that is, Origen thought that there was an arguable case for reincarnation which merited submission to the judgement of his readers. The statements of Philo and even Clement (above, p. 143, n. 90) would have led them to expect something on the subject.

(70) Pamphilus, *Apol.* (XXIV. 405–12 Lommatzsch). Pamphilus's preface is of great importance for his view of Origen's 'inquiries' and the implications of Origen's exploratory attitude for the nature of Christian doctrinal affirmations.

(71) *Dial. c. Heracl.* 1st ed., p. 166.

(72) *c. Cels.* iii. 81, 'Do not suppose that it is not consistent with Christian doctrine when in my reply to Celsus I accepted the opinions of those philosophers who have affirmed the immortality or the survival of the soul. We have some ideas in common with them.'

(73) *c. Cels.* iii. 40; *Exh. Mart.* 47. Cf. Gregory Thaumaturgus, *Paneg.* 2. 13.

(74) *c. Cels.* vi. 43; cf. iv. 40, where he says that the doctrine of Genesis iii has a 'mysterious meaning superior to the Platonic doctrine' of *Phaedrus* 246 c.

(75) Undeterred by the obvious similarity to the trichotomist view of the cosmos associated with the Valentinians, Origen (like Philo) very frequently affirms that the *psyche* stands midway between the material body and the divine *pneuma*, pulled in both directions and free to choose which it will have as its associate. The soul that associates with the body and cherishes its appetites becomes carnal, but the soul that is united to the *pneuma* is joined to the Lord and ascends to deification. Cf. *de Princ.* ii. 8; ii. 10. 1; 10. 7; *Comm. in Rom.* ii. 9; *in Matt. Ser.* 57; *Comm. in Joh.* i. 2. 9, and the references at p. 151, n. 35. The doctrine was held by some of the late commentators on the *Timaeus*, where Plato says that God set the soul 'in the middle' (34 B). Porphyry, Iamblichus, and Proclus strongly criticize those who took Plato's words in a spatial sense, as if the world-soul were located in the centre of the earth, or in the moon 'as if it were the neck connecting the created and divine realms', or in the sun. Porphyry (frag. 61 Sodano = Proclus, *in Tim.* II. 104–5 Diehl) interprets Plato to mean that *psyche* stands midway metaphysically between intelligible and sensible realities. Proclus regularly takes the same view (*in Tim.* I. 402 f.; II. 1, 102, 158, 282, etc.). But he formally rejects the view (taken by some Platonists he does not name) that the soul is 'of one substance' with the divine souls and rises to become wholly *nous*, leaving all soulness behind (III. 231, 245). This rejected view closely resembles Origen's.

(76) *de Princ.* i. 7. 4; 9. 7; iii. 3. 5; 5. 5.

(77) *de Princ.* ii. 9. 3–8. Origen even explains differences of intellectual ability by the hypothesis that the bodiless minds not only fell

different distances from God but are also more or less 'psychic' or dense in strict accord with their merit (ii. 8. 4).

(78) *de Princ.* i. 7. 4; iii. 3. 5.

(79) The question is listed in the preface to *de Principiis* as one to which the apostolic tradition gives no authoritative answer. The chief discussion occurs in the commentary on the Song of Songs (ii, p. 147 Baehrens), where he reviews the Traducianist opinion that the substance of the soul is contained in the bodily seed, the Creationist opinion that the necessity of animating the conceived embryo is the cause of the soul's creation, and whether the notion of pre-existence necessarily implies transmigration and a doctrine of world-cycles. Origen thought that the embryo receives its soul at conception from an angel presiding over the birth (*Comm. in Joh.* xiii. 50), an opinion also held by the unnamed presbyter quoted by Clement, *Ecl. Proph.* 50. In *Comm. in Matt.* xv. 35 Origen argues generally for pre-existence against the alternative view, common to both Creationist and Traducianist, that the soul and body come into existence simultaneously. Tertullian (*de Anima* 27) shows how fear of gnostic myths about transmigration played a large part in arousing fear of the pre-existence theory. Nevertheless, in a remarkable discussion (*de Natura Hominis* ii. 17, *P.G.* 40. 571 ff.), Nemesius of Emesa concludes that the objections to Creationism and Traducianism are too great for their acceptance. Nemesius, however, disavows Origen's notion of ascending and descending ranks of souls (iii. 22, *P.G.* 40. 608 A—the sentence is irrelevant to what precedes and follows, and looks like an afterthought, if not a later or misplaced insertion in the text).

(80) *Rep.* 617 E ff. insists that souls choose their condition of life and that God is not responsible (cf. *Tim.* 42 D; *Phaedrus* 249 B).

(81) *de Orat.* 24. 3; *Comm. in Joh.* xx. 7. 52–53. Cf. Gregory Thaumaturgus, *Paneg.* 8. 113; Jerome, *in Eph.* i. 17. (Jerome's commentary on Ephesians, as the catenae show, very largely reproduces the lost commentary of Origen and is for the most part to be treated as a paraphrastic abridgement, not as an independent work.)

(82) *c. Cels.* v. 29.

(83) *Comm. in Joh.* vi. 13. 74, where he is meeting the gnostic appeal to the gospel saying that John the Baptist is Elijah come again (for

which cf. J. H. Waszink's full commentary on Tertullian, *de Anima* 35. 5).

(84) *c. Cels.* iv. 83.

(85) Plato, *Phaedo* 80 B; cf. *Rep.* 612 A. On this question of reincarnation in animals the later Platonists came to be divided. Plato's words were clear enough, and Numenius of Apamea accepted the doctrine (Aeneas of Gaza reports him so, *P.G.* 85. 892 B). Plotinus also did so, while showing an awareness of the existence of objections (iii. 4. 2; iv. 3. 12; vi. 7. 6–7), some of which appear as early as Lucretius (iii. 748 ff.). The force of the criticism, however, was especially felt by Porphyry, who at one time accepted Plotinus's view (Stobaeus i. 49. 60; Nemesius, *de Nat. Hom.* 2. 18, *P.G.* 40. 583 A) and at another rejected it in favour of the view that Plato wrote figuratively and that rational souls only become reincarnate in human bodies (Augustine, *de Civ. Dei* x. 30; xii. 26; xiii. 19; Aeneas of Gaza, *P.G.* 85. 893 A). Probably because the latter view was supported by the high authority of the Chaldean Oracles (Proclus, *in Remp.* II. 336, 27 Kroll), it became the normal view for Iamblichus (Nemesius, *P.G.* 40. 483 A; Aeneas, *P.G.* 85. 893 A), Sallustius (*de Diis et mundo* 20), Hierocles (in Photius, *Bibl.* 214 and 251), and the Hermetic writers (*Corp. Herm.* x. 19). Proclus (*in Tim.* III. 294 f.) produces a formula of compromise that, even while brought down to a beast's level through its low sympathies, yet the soul transcends this level in itself and does not actually occupy an animal body. On the problem of Porphyry's opinion cf. H. Dörrie, 'Kontroversen um die Seelenwanderung im kaiserzeitlichen Platonismus', in *Hermes* 85 (1957), 414–35.

(86) See the discussion of the age of the earth in, e.g., Macrobius, *in Somn. Scip.* ii. 10. 5–16: Who could suppose the earth has always existed when civilization is of such recent growth? That it has always existed is certain on philosophical grounds; so the explanation lies in the almost complete destruction of the race by periodic catastrophes of water and fire. The fountain-head of these ideas is *Tim.* 22 D, 39 D, and *Politicus* 269 A ff. Cf. above ch. 1, p. 11.

(87) The best collection of evidence with discussion is given by W. L. Knox, *St. Paul and the Church of the Gentiles* (Cambridge, 1939), pp. 4 ff.

(88) *Comm. in Cant. Cantic.* iii (p. 210 Baehrens); *c. Cels.* i. 20 (not yet 10,000); iv. 79. Cf. Augustine, *de Civ. Dei* xii. 10–11.

(89) e.g. *de Princ.* i. 2. 10; 4. 3–4. Methodius criticizes Origen's use of this argument as insufficiently safeguarding the freedom of God (*de Creatis* 2, p. 494 Bonwetsch = Photius, *Bibl.* 235, 302 a, 30 ff.).

(90) *de Princ.* ii. 9. 1; iii. 5. 2; iv. 4. 8; *Comm. in Matt.* xiii. 1.

(91) Sallustius, *de Diis et mundo* 20. That the argument played some part in Porphyry's commentary on the *Timaeus* is a deduction from Calcidius, *in Tim.* 148, printed in Sodano's edition of the fragments of Porphyry (Naples, 1964), p. 83 f.

(92) Augustine, *de Civ. Dei* xii. 17 ff.

(93) Aeneas of Gaza, *P.G.* 85. 953 where, to Theophrastus's invocation of the argument that a finite world implies a recurrent cycle with transmigrating souls, Aeneas retorts that the doctrine of a finite number of souls is 'more mine than yours'. Philoponus (cf. his *de Aeternitate mundi c. Proclum* i. 2–3) is attacked by Simplicius, *in Aristot. Phys.* VIII, 1 (pp. 1179 ff. Diels).

The logical problem is related to the question of the Platonic schools whether the number of Forms is finite or infinite (see E. R. Dodds, *Proclus, the Elements of Theology*, pp. 246–50). Plotinus (v. 7 (18). 1) remarks that the soul contains all that is in the world but not infinity, and therefore there must be periodic cycles. Plotinus's pupil Amelius held that there is indeed an infinity of forms which may require 'more than an infinity of time' for realization (Syrianus, *in Metaph.* p. 147, 1 ff.). Syrianus and his pupil Proclus (*Dubia* 2; i, p. 98 f. Cousin) hold that the Forms are not infinite in number, but seem so to us. According to Proclus finite and infinite are relative terms: what is infinite to inferior beings is finite to superior beings, and nothing can be infinite to itself without being incomprehensible to itself.

(94) Theophilus Alex., *Ep. pasch.* 2. 17 (= Jerome, *Ep.* 98. 17); Justinian, *Edictum contra Origenem* (*A.C.O.* III. 209, excerpt ii; cf. 190, 8–14). Origen could evidently have replied that intrinsic impossibilities do not fall within the omnipotence of God.

(95) *Hom. in Lev.* vii. 2.

(96) *de Princ.* iv. 4. 9; *Hom. in Gen.* xiii. 4; *c. Cels.* ii. 11, and many passages rejecting the gnostic doctrine of total depravity.

(97) *c. Cels.* iii. 69; viii. 72; *Comm. in Joh.* xx. 5 and 28.

(98) *c. Cels.* vii. 44; *de Orat.* 29. 19; *Philocalia* 25 (from *Comm. in Rom.* i. 3); especially *Comm. in Rom.* vii. 7–8.

(99) *in Matt. Ser.* 56.

(100) Besides his influence on the principles of Biblical exegesis, Philo directly anticipates Origen in the doctrine that souls fall as a result of a satiety with divine contemplation (above, p. 151, n. 34). He also shares Origen's idea of revelation as divine accommodation (*Somn.* i. 232 f.), so that God means different things to people at different stages of spiritual advance (*Mut. Nom.* 19 ff.). Both men explain the Biblical 'wrath of God' as remedial (e.g. *Det. Pot.* 144 ff.; *Qu. Gen.* i. 73; iv. 51; *Immut.* 52–69), like a physician who applies his medicines gradually lest too speedy a recovery endanger the patient's lasting health (*Qu. Ex.* ii. 25; cf. Origen, *de Princ.* iii. 1. 13; *de Orat.* 29. 16; *Philocalia* 27 from *Comm. in Exod.*). A theme paradoxically more prominent in Origen than in Philo is that the mystical ascent is unending, never static. Cf. *Hom. in Num.* xvii. 4; xxvii. 12; prol. *in Cant. Cantic.* (p. 79 Baehrens); *de Princ.* ii. 3. 7; iv. 3. 14 (citing Phil. iii. 14); *de Orat.* 25. 2 (gnosis is never possession, but ceaseless advance).

(101) *Panarion haer.* 67. 7. 4.

(102) Cf. Justinian, *contra Origenem*, A.C.O. III. 191, 1 ff. = *P.G.* 86. 949 B: 'Like other heretics Origen mixes pieces of orthodox doctrine with his wicked writings, but these belong not to him but to the holy Church of God. He did this with a malicious intention to deceive the simple.'

(103) *Hom. in Jerem.* xx. 4.

(104) Cf. F. Hockey's demonstration (*Rev. Bénéd.* 72 (1962), 349–50) that the Rule of St. Benedict (25–28) depends on Origen's 7th Homily on Joshua. In the *Regula Magistri* xi Origen is quoted with high reverence as 'Origenes sapiens' (admittedly the sentence quoted is from the maxims of Sextus). The reference for the allusion to Origen in *The Ancrene Riwle* (transl. M. B. Salu, 1955), p. 104, is *Hom. in Jesu* xv. 6. On the remarkable extent to which

Origen was admiringly read in the West during the Middle Ages see H. de Lubac, *Exégèse médiévale* 1. i, pp. 221–304.

(105) Basil, *de Spiritu sancto* xxix. 73 (written perhaps very soon after a perusal of Epiphanius's indictment in the *Panarion*).

(106) *Comm. in Joh.* xx. 30; xxxii. 16.

(107) *Comm. in Gen.*, cited in the preface to Pamphilus's Apology (XXIV. 296 Lommatzsch).

(108) Letter to John Eck, 15 May 1518 (*Ep.* 844, III, p. 337 Allen): 'Plus me docet Christianae philosophiae unica Origenis pagina quam decem Augustini.'

INDEX

Adoptianists, 51, 130.
Aelian, 36.
Aeneas of Gaza, 118, 167 f.
Albinus, 128, 152, 163.
Alexander of Lycopolis, 136.
Allegory, 6, 27, 73–76, 97–98, 111 f., 156 f.
Ambrose of Milan, 129.
Ambrose, patron of Origen, 73, 100, 138.
Amelius, 15, 168.
Ammonius Saccas, 68 f., 109.
Anamnesis, 115.
Ancrene Riwle, 169.
Andresen, C., 131–3.
Animals, 106; transmigration to, 169.
Anthologies, 35, 37, 160.
Antinous, 11.
Apollinarianism, 153.
Aratus, 43.
Aristophanes, 160.
Aristotle, 39, 41, 43, 108–11.
Asclepius, 38.
Athanasius, 158.
Athenaeus, 36.
Athenagoras, 47.
Atticus, Platonist, 108–10.
Attis, 6.
Augustine, 14, 16, 87, 118, 129, 137.
Authority, 52, 80.

Baptism, infant, 90.
Bardy, G., 132, 162.
Barth, P., 162.
Basil of Caesarea, 122, 149, 170.
Bauer, W., 138.
Benedict, Rule of, 169.

Benz, E., 128.
Berdyaev, N., 96.
Bible, 53 f., 64, 70–76, 82, 112.
Böhringer, F., 149.
Bousset, W., 33.
Browne, Thomas, 2.
Buckley, E. R., 125.
Buddhism, 32.
Butterworth, G. W., 149.

Calcidius, 168.
Calder, W. M., 125.
Campenhausen, H. von, 125, 148, 154, 164.
Candidus, Valentinian, 99.
Cassiodorus, 155.
Cavallera, F., 156.
Celibacy, 90.
Celsus, 22–30, 34, 49, 65.
Chaldean Oracles, 167.
Christ, 16–18, 56; atonement, 144; descent to Hades, 45, eternal generation, 84; incarnation, 50 f., 76 f., 91 f., 111, 157, 164; sinlessness, 90; virgin birth, 90, 123, 131, 133. See also Logos.
Chrysippus, 107, 160.
Clement of Alexandria, 1, 5, 8–10, 15, 31–66, 73, 75, 101–3, 106.
Coleridge, S. T., 104.
Constantine, 17.
Cook, A. B., 126.
Cosmetics, 62.
Crantor, 160.
Creation, 12, 44–48, 57 f., 83–89, 128.
Creationism, 115.
Crescens, 10.

Critolaus, 163.
Cross, F. L., 155.
Crouzel, H., 96, 162.
Cybele, 6, 29.
Cyril of Scythopolis, 155.

Daniélou, J., 96, 128, 150.
Dante, 151.
Demetrius of Alexandria, 69, 99 f.
Didymus of Alexandria, 96.
Diekamp, F., 155.
Dihle, A., 138.
Dionysus, as God of the Jews, 7; cult, 29, 38.
Dodds, E. R., 132, 149, 168.
Dörrie, H., 149, 167.
Downey, G., 160

Eclecticism, 5, 21 f., 30, 40 f.
Edsman, C. M., 145.
Epictetus, 107.
Epicurus, 39, 132.
Epimenides, 43.
Epiphanius, 8, 100 f., 121 f., 155, 159, 170.
Erasmus, 123.
Eriugena, Scotus, 96.
Eroticism, 58, 62.
Ethics, 41–43, 58–63, 90 f., 104 f.
Eunapius, 69.
Euripides, 37, 39, 160.
Eusebius of Caesarea, 31, 66–68.
Evagrius Ponticus, 96, 121.
Evil, 88 f., 136.

Fabian of Rome, 100.
Faith, 39, 51–54.
Fascher, E., 128.
Festugière, A.-J., 155, 162 f.
Fishing, 62.
Florus of Lyons, 127.

Galen, 160.

Geffcken, J., 131.
Geytenbeek, A. C., 147.
Gnilka, J., 154.
Gnosticism, 7 f., 19, 21, 33 f., 53, 72, 82, 88, 90, 99, 112, 119.
God, freedom, 120; *hypsistos*, 125; nameless, 125, 150; omnipotent, 118, 168; Trinity, 15, 92, 108, 151; transcendent, 15 f., 21, 28; God of Jews, 7, 25, 125 f.
Goodenough, E. R., 126. 132.
Grace, 54–56, 108.
Grant, R. M., 127, 150.
Gregory of Nazianzus, 126, 149, 155, 163.
Gregory of Nyssa, 162.
Gregory Thaumaturgus, 156, 165 f.
Guillaumont, A., 155.

Hadrian, 11.
Hanson, R. P. C., 150.
Harder, R., 126.
Harl, M., 139, 149.
Harnack, A. von, 128. 135, 157.
Hell, 78.
Heraclas, 70.
Heracleon, 73.
Heracles, 38.
Heraclides, bishop, 114.
Heraclitus, 15, 23.
Hermas, Shepherd of, 45.
Hermogenes, 47.
Hexapla, 70 f.
Hierocles, neoplatonist, 69, 152.
Hippolytus, 8.
Homer, 6, 37, 103.
Horace, 102.
Hornschuh, M., 148.,

Iamblichus, 163, 165, 167.
Iao, 125.
Irenaeus, 9, 40, 47, 50, 56, 79, 81 f.
Isis, 6.

Jerome, 79. 86 f., 149.
John, St., 73.
John of Damascus, 126.
Josephus, 13, 128.
Judaism, 6 f., 13, 23, 26, 30, 40, 131.
Julian, emperor, 118.
Justin Martyr, 4, 9–23, 30, 32, 40 f., 44 f., 64, 79, 101, 103, 106, 124–34.
Justinian, 96, 118, 120, 149, 155, 168 f.
Juvenal, 35.

Keys, power of, 93, 154.
Kierkegaard, S., 2.
Klostermann, E., 163.
Knox, W. L., 167.
Köster, H., 125.
Koetschau, P., 121, 149, 154.

Labarum, 17.
Labhard, A., 124.
Langerbeck, H., 149.
Leemans, E. A., 132.
Lewy, H., 146.
Lippelt, E., 125.
Logos, 4, 16, 24, 39, 51, 57, 94, 103 f. *See also* Christ.
Lubac, H. de, 96, 151, 170.
Lucian of Samosata, 20 f., 52, 132, 134.
Lutz, C. E., 147.

Macrobius, 167.
Marcellus of Ancyra, 155 f., 159.
Marcion, 26.
Marrou, H.-I., 138 f.
Maximus of Tyre, 132.
Melito of Sardis, 164.
Menander, 37, 39, 43.
Mercati, G., 154.
Methodius, 79.
Millennium, 19, 78 f.

Minucius Felix, 137.
Miracles, 17, 144.
Mithras, 6.
Modalism, 92.
Money, 61.
Moses, 13 f.
Munck, J., 138.
Musonius, 60, 107.

Nautin, P., 138.
Nemesius of Emesa, 166 f.
Neopythagoreanism, 14 f., 64, 68, 147.
Nicolas of Cusa, 96.
Nock, A. D., 128, 133.
Numenius, 15, 20–22, 68, 129, 167.

Origen, 1, 9 f., 66–123, 148–70.
Orthodoxy, 32, 34, 79 f., 96 ff.
Orwell, George, 53.
Osiris as God of Jews, 125.
Ovid, 151.

Pamphilus, 67, 114, 164, 170.
Pantaenus, 32 f., 137 f.
Paul, St., 3, 7 f., 35, 43, 50, 74, 76; married, 59.
Paul of Samosata, 156.
Pease, A. S., 128.
Petronius, 35.
Philo, 4–7, 11, 13, 40 f., 44–46, 55–57, 75 f., 86, 90, 98, 120, 128 f., 140–3, 150–2, 169.
Photius, 47, 49, 126.
Physiologus, 107.
Pico della Mirandola, 96.
Plagiarism, 13–15, 23 f., 35, 43 f.
Plato, biography, 14, read by Clement, 37; philosophical ideas, 5–7, 11 f., 14 f., 21–23, 27–30, 39, 41, 44–46, 57–59, 72, 79, 81–83, 85–86, 88, 111–18, 122, 128 f.

Philoponus, 168.
Plotinus, 8, 167 f.
Plutarch, 125, 160.
Pohlenz, M., 140.
Porphyry, 66–69, 103, 118, 129, 137, 161, 163, 165, 167.
Prayer, 54, 63, 113.
Predestination, 119.
Pre-existence, 115. *See also* Soul.
Proclus, neoplatonist, 124, 156, 165, 167 f.
Providence, 88 f., 106–8, 115.
Puech, A., 131.
Puech, H.-C., 126, 132.
Purgatory, 55, 78, 93 f.

Refoulé, R. F., 132.
Reitzenstein, R., 129.
Resurrection, 19, 78 f., 87, 110 f.; spherical bodies, 151.
Richardson, C. C., 129, 159.
Rufinus, 12, 149.

Sallustius, 167.
Salu, M. B., 169.
Sanday, W., 125.
Satan, 44, 80 f., 93 f., 99 f., 158; not inventor of logic, 140.
Saturn, as God of the Jews, 7.
Schleiermacher, F. D. E., 104.
Schmid, W., 131.
Schmidt, C., 126.
Schneemelcher, W., 124, 159.
Schnitzer, K. F., 148.
Scholarius, 95.
Schürer, E., 126.
Schwartz, E., 124.
Seneca, 35, 61, 151, 160.
Sex, 37, 58–60, 89 f.
Simon, M., 137.
Simonetti, M., 158.
Simplicius, neoplatonist, 168.

Sin, 90 f.
Socrates, 16 f., 128.
Sodano, A. R., 161.
Soul, 48 f., 85, 111–16.
Spanneut, M., 131.
Sparks, H. F. D., 125.
Stage, 61.
Stobaeus, 36.
Stoicism, 5 f., 11, 16, 21, 30, 32, 39, 41, 43, 46, 49, 63, 82, 104–8.
Stone, D., 96.
Strycker, É. de, 125.
Syncretism, 7, 21, 26.
Syrian goddess, 6.
Syrianus, 162, 168.

Tatian, 15, 32, 125, 127, 137.
Tertullian, 1 f., 64, 124.
Theodoret, 126, 164.
Theophilus of Alexandria, 118.
Thraede, K., 141.
Traducianism, 115.
Transmigration, 49, 114–16.
Tresmontant, C., 132.

Universalism, 118–20.

Valentinianism, 34, 72 f., 141, 165.
Varro, 125, 162.
Victorinus, Marius, 3.
Völker, W., 135, 140.

Waszink, J. H., 124, 142, 151.
Weber, H. O., 149.
Wifstrand, A., 134.
Wilson, R. McL., 124.
Wind, E., 155.
Wine, 60.
World, eternal, 116–18.

Zahn, T., 124.
Zeus Sabazius, 125.